Deli~~ght~~
Woman *of* Wonder

Devotional Bible study spiritual warfare handbook for today's women of God with practical, effective strategies for victory over darkness in the battlefield of the mind

By Mikaela Vincent

Fight evil and win!

Put on the armor of God, victorious warrior, and fight for your marriage and family. Overcome conflict, fear, anxiety, and strongholds with these battle tactics for living in Christ's power. Best seller war room prayer manual for breaking free.

Step into the adventure...
Mikaela Vincent
More Than A Conqueror Books
We're not just about books. We're about books that make a difference in the lives of those you care about.

www.MoreThanAConquerorBooks.com

Follow, friend, like Mikaela Vincent, and share with your friends:
Facebook Page: **Mikaela.Vincent.author**
Facebook Profile: **Mikaela.Vincent.MoreThanAConquerorBooks**
Instagram: **Mikaela.Vincent**
Twitter: **Mikaela_Vincent**
Pinterest: **Mikaela Vincent: More Than A Conqueror Books**
Blog: **www.MoreThanAConquerorBooks.wordpress.com**

Copyright © 2017 by Mikaela Vincent
More Than A Conqueror Books
MoreThanAConquerorBooks@gmail.com
www.MoreThanAConquerorBooks.com

All Scripture quotations, unless otherwise indicated, are taken from the Holy Bible, New International Version®, NIV®. Copyright ©1973, 1978, 1984, 2011 by Biblica, Inc.™ Used by permission of Zondervan. All rights reserved worldwide. www.zondervan.com The "NIV" and "New International Version" are trademarks registered in the United States Patent and Trademark Office by Biblica, Inc.™

Delight to Be a Woman of Wonder Power Planner

A powerful day planner to accompany *Delight to Be a Woman of Wonder*

by Mikaela Vincent

Burnout happens when you're doing more than God has asked you to, or you're doing it in your own power. Let God be your Time Manager with this day planner designed to hand all your plans to Christ, and walk in His power every moment. (See Strategies 34-37 in this book.) Includes tips for hearing God's voice and walking in His Spirit.

Available with or without lines, dated or undated.

Delight to Be a Woman of Wonder Prayer Journal

by Mikaela Vincent

Accompanies all the strategies in this book.

A beautiful prayer journal notebook diary for guided conversations with your King, including war room prayer prompts for overcoming the enemy, special love letters from your Beloved, and room to write in.

www.MoreThanAConquerorBooks.com

(All proceeds the author receives go to sharing the Light in dark areas of the world where few have ever heard of Christ.)

If you would like to pray through and practice these spiritual warfare strategies together with your husband, these books are for him:

Dare to Be a Mighty Warrior

by Mikaela Vincent

Mirrors each strategy in this book, only written uniquely for the man of God to walk out in his spiritual authority as a husband, father, and friend of Christ, protecting and blessing his family, as he listens to God's voice and walks as one with Him and with his wife, family, and others he is responsible for.

Dare to Be a Mighty Warrior Prayer Journal

by Mikaela Vincent

Accompanies the *Dare to Be a Mighty Warrior* spiritual warfare handbook

Guided conversations with the King for freedom from strongholds, protecting the ones you love, listening to God's voice, removing barriers to oneness, and fulfilling your purpose as a man of God, husband, father, and friend of Christ. Available with or without lines.

Available with or without lines.
www.MoreThanAConquerorBooks.com

To all you beautiful women of God, who valiantly fight life's battles in your marriage, family, workplace, world, and especially in your own mind and heart ...

Finally, be strong in the Lord and in His mighty power. Put on the full armor of God, so that you can take your stand against the devil's schemes. For our struggle is not against flesh and blood, but against the rulers, against the authorities, against the powers of this dark world and against the spiritual forces of evil in the heavenly realms. Therefore put on the full armor of God, so that when the day of evil comes, you may be able to stand your ground, and after you have done everything, to stand. Stand firm then, with the belt of truth buckled around your waist, with the breastplate of righteousness in place, and with your feet fitted with the readiness that comes from the gospel of peace. In addition to all this, take up the shield of faith, with which you can extinguish all the flaming arrows of the evil one. Take the helmet of salvation and the sword of the Spirit, which is the word of God. And pray in the Spirit on all occasions with all kinds of prayers and requests. With this in mind, be alert and always keep on praying for all the Lord's people. **Pray also for me, that whenever I speak, words may be given me so that I will fearlessly make known the mystery of the gospel.**

Ephesians 6:10-20

Don't be in a hurry to make it through the 100 battle strategies for victory in this book. Take your time. Let the Lord teach you, bring the circumstances into your life that fit practicing what you're learning, and empower you to overcome. Whether or not your circumstances change, **when you draw near to Christ,** *you* **change.** *And that changes everything!*

Strategies for Victory

1. Let Jesus be Lord	10
2. Know what you're fighting for	11
3. Know why we are at war	12
4. Love: the greatest Power	13
5. Know the Truth	14
6. Let Jesus take the lead	15
7. Wear your armor	16
8. Know the targets to demolish	17
9. Remove the barriers	18
10. The James 4 Principle	19
11. Live Kingdom Culture	20
12. The Three-Fold Sieve	21
13. The Galatians Gauge	22
14. Follow the feelings to the lies	23
15. Recognize strongholds	24
16. Remove guardian lies	25
17. Scrub off the whitewash	26
18. Truth Encounter	27
19. Picture freedom. Stay free.	28

20. Repulsed by your sin	29
21. Refill the empty places	30
22. Linked healing	31
23. Break unholy vows	32
24. One with your sword	33
25. Handling your sword	34
26. Your sword's Name	35
27. Live by the sword	36
28. Word Search	37
29. Daily quiet times	38
30. Personal spiritual retreats	39
31. Listen UP before deciding	40
32. Body structure	41
33. Modeling body structure	42
34. Let God be Time Manager	43
35. First thought: Jesus	44
36. Lord of the day	45
37. Lord of the night	46
38. Protection prayer	47
39. Cleanse that nightmare	48
40. Philippians 4 Plan for Peace	49
41. Trust God's sovereignty	50
42. Turn to God, not away	51
43. Look for God's plan	52
44. Go opposite Satan's plan	53
45. Come up here	54
46. Wreck it in Jesus' arms	55

47. Don't get distracted	56
48. Distracted by God	57
49. Hunger for God	58
50. Fear of the Lord	59
51. Don't listen to fear	60
52. Out you go, Fear!	61
53. Stronghold domino effect	62
54. Let grace free you	63
55. Recognize pride's chains	64
56. Let humility release you	65
57. Lay down pride and listen	66
58. Fight for others' freedom	67
59. End to conflict starts in me	68
60. Get alone. Get Truth	69
61. Truth set-up	70
62. Truth Counselor	71
63. Lay down yours, pick up His	72
64. Fight for your brother	73
65. No mind-reading	74
66. Change me first	75
67. The Matthew 18:15 Principle	76
68. Humbly ask forgiveness	77
69. Do everything in love	78
70. Forgive	79
71. Freedom through forgiveness	80
72. Plead for mercy	81
73. Curses turned blessings	82

74. Break off curses	83
75. Know and live your purpose	84
76. Speak blessings, not curses	85
77. Guard your mouth!	86
78. Eternal mindset	87
79. From mundane to mighty	88
80. Expect God	89
81. Let God lead the conversation	90
82. Seek God's instructions	91
83. Reject what's not from God	92
84. Lord, how do You see me?	93
85. "If this is the enemy, stop it!"	94
86. Pray for eternal things	95
87. Offensive strategy	96
88. Break soul ties	97
89. Build protective hedges	98
90. Cloak of transparency	99
91. Don't cause others to fall	100
92. Renounce occult activity	101
93. "Go! And don't come back!"	102
94. Cleanse your home	103
95. Break generational curses	104
96. Free your children to be free	105
97. Pray in your authority	106
98. Walk in your authority	107
99. Worship intercession	108
100. Be still	109

1 Victory Strategy

Let Jesus be Lord

Ephesians 6:12; John 3:16; 10:10; Ephesians 2:8

HEART CHECKLIST

As you practice the strategies for overcoming evil in this handbook, pray through this running checklist on the side for God to expose any wrong thought processes, sins, or other barriers to oneness with Him. As He leads, use the Truth Encounter in Strategy 18 and/or the Word Search in Strategy 28 for deeper freedom, especially from thoughts and reactions that keep coming back, even when you try to repent. Write your experiences with God in your journal.

You are in a real battle with a real enemy. You don't get to skip it if you're a Christian, but **you *are* on the winning side.**

If you're not a Christian, you didn't just pick up this book by chance. **God is drawing you to Himself.** He created you to know Him and enjoy His great love for you, but wrong choices have separated you from His purposes and set you on a deadly path. If you keep heading that way, you'll miss out on the wonder-filled life He planned for you, and face eternal death.

But God loves you and has provided a way for you to be forgiven and reunited to His love. His Son Jesus took your place and died for your sin. Then He rose again so you could have eternal life. The salvation He offers you is free, and **He is inviting you to enjoy love, peace, and joy in His presence now,** and **eternal life with Him in Heaven, where every tear is washed away**. But like any gift, **you must receive it for it to be yours**.

You can do that by believing what Jesus has done for you, turning away from your sin, and inviting Him to be Lord over your life. If the chains of your sin feel too powerful to break free, know that **you're not meant to do it alone; Jesus holds the keys to your freedom**. But first, you must invite Him in: *"Jesus, I believe You died for me and rose again so I could be free. Please forgive me of my sin, and be Lord over my life. I want to know You and follow Your ways for my life...."*

Some of you reading this said a prayer like that years ago but haven't really let Jesus be Lord over your life. You're still doing things your own bobbling way, missing out on the abundant life God planned for you.

Revelation 2:4-5

☐ *forsaking Christ as my First Love*

☐ _____

☐ _____

> ARE THERE ANY AREAS OF YOUR LIFE YOU HAVEN'T GIVEN TO JESUS YET? IN YOUR JOURNAL, WRITE A PRAYER, INVITING HIM TO BE LORD OVER ALL YOUR LIFE.
>
> AS YOU PRACTICE THE STRATEGIES IN THIS BOOK, PRAY THROUGH THE CHECKLIST ON THE SIDES TO UNCOVER ENEMY SCHEMES THAT HINDER ONENESS WITH CHRIST. LET JESUS TAKE YOU ON A JOURNEY TO FREEDOM.

Know what you're fighting for

Victory strategy 2

2 Corinthians 10:3-5; 1 Peter 5:6-11, James 2:19

The father of lies (John 8:44) is waging war to draw you away from Truth (John 14:6). The battle is not for things to go your way, for you to be treated right, to convince others to agree with you, or to get people to do what you want.

> **This war is for oneness with Christ.**
>> **Your enemy is Satan** and his forces.
>>> The **battlefield is your heart and mind.**
>>>> And the **stakes are eternal.**

You were not created to get beaten up in this fight, but to stand strong in Christ's power, *to love God, feel His great love for you, and bring Him glory by loving others through His love.* Ephesians 6:10-20, Matthew 22:37-40.

Even so, *if you are not on the alert, you could fall prey to enemy schemes.* 1 Peter 5:8. The good news is **the Sovereign One Who loves you, fights for you, and arms you to win is *all-powerful*.** To walk in the fullness of the truth and authority He has given you (John 14:15-17), start by *knowing who you are in Christ.**

Forge ahead, victorious warrior. The battle will not wait!

Revelation 2:4-5 ...
- ☐ wanting these more than Christ:
- ☐ entertainment
- ☐ work
- ☐ ambition
- ☐ money
- ☐ busyness
- ☐ pleasing others
- ☐ feelings
- ☐ sin
- ☐ approval
- ☐ pleasure
- ☐ comfort
- ☐ people
- ☐ _____
- ☐ _____
- ☐ _____
- ☐ _____
- ☐ _____
- ☐ _____
- ☐ _____
- ☐ _____

> IN WHAT WAYS HAVE YOU FELT BEATEN UP IN THIS FIGHT, RATHER THAN A VICTORIOUS WARRIOR? JOURNAL YOUR ANSWER TO THE LORD, AND THEN WRITE A PRAYER BASED ON 2 CORINTHIANS 12:9-10, ASKING GOD TO OVERCOME YOUR WEAKNESSES.
>
> LOOK UP THE FOLLOWING PASSAGES, AND BEGIN A LIST IN YOUR JOURNAL OF WHO YOU ARE IN CHRIST, ADDING TO IT AS GOD SHOWS YOU MORE IN YOUR DAILY TIMES WITH HIM: JOHN 15:15; 1 CORINTHIANS 6:19; 12:27; HEBREWS 10:14; GALATIANS 5:13; PSALM 103:12; EPHESIANS 2:10; 1 CORINTHIANS 3:9; ACTS 1:8; MATTHEW 5:14; 2 CORINTHIANS 5:20; EPHESIANS 2:19.

**Delight to Be a Woman of God*, by Mikaela Vincent, offers Bible studies on knowing who you are in Christ, unlocking your beauty, walking as one with the One you love, and becoming who He created you to be. Available at www.MoreThanAConquerorBooks.com

3 Victory Strategy — Know why we are at war

Ephesians 6:10-20; Revelation 12; Hebrews 10:14

Psalm 40

- ☐ not trusting God
- ☐ trusting in prideful people who seek after selfish idols
- ☐ unfulfilled vows
- ☐ "serving" God without true surrender
- ☐ closing my ears to God's words
- ☐ sealing my lips, not testifying about God to others
- ☐ concealing God's love and truth
- ☐ not standing up for righteousness
- ☐ letting sin overtake or control me
- ☐ desiring the ruin of a servant of Christ or Christian leader
- ☐ seeking to destroy the reputation of someone who loves God
- ☐ not seeking God

When Satan, formerly an angel in God's service, proudly waged war against the Most High, he and his followers were thrown out of Heaven. Now, because God lovingly created each of us for relationship with Him, Satan and his demons wage war against us to draw us away from that love. Revelation 12.

A dreadful tale, especially for those of us who have felt the heat of Satan's anger. But our enemy actually is already defeated. The trials you experience now, in some respects, are just the tail thrashing about after the serpent's head has been cut off. 1 Corinthians 15:1-4, 20-23, 51-58.

So, if Jesus has already won the victory through His death and resurrection, why are we still fighting? Because *we are in the process of "being made holy."* Hebrews 10:14.

You aren't here on earth to be comfortable, make an empire for yourself, get everyone to like you, or do what you want. **You're here to draw near to God and to influence others to do the same.**

This time we have on earth is training ground. It's where we experience God's character, love, grace, holiness, and power; and make choices moment-by-moment about what or whom we will love and serve. Those who choose Christ and endure to the end receive the prize. Hebrews 12:1-3.

If we were all mindless robots serving God because we had to, there would be no fight, no reason for Satan to bother us. In fact, we wouldn't exist at all. Because God is Almighty, All-powerful. He doesn't need to create a bunch of people to do something *for* Him. He can do *anything*. Rather, He created us for *relationship*, **to love Him, enjoy Him, and draw others into that love.**

Those who don't choose God's side don't get to skip the fight; they just miss out on the joy and peace that come from going through each battle in Christ's empowering. Exodus 14:14.

> IN WHAT WAYS HAVE YOU RECOGNIZED YOU ARE IN A BATTLE BETWEEN LIGHT AND DARKNESS? WRITE THOSE THOUGHTS IN YOUR JOURNAL, AND WRITE A LETTER TO YOUR KING, RECOMMITTING FEALTY TO HIM.

Love: the greatest Power

Victory strategy 4

2 Corinthians 10:3-5; John 16:33; 1 John 4:4

You have a real enemy. But it's not your brother. So whatever you're fighting about, take a step back and look at what the issue really is. What is Satan trying to do? What part does he want you to play in this battle?

God is calling you to humility, love, grace, truth, and most importantly, *greater oneness with Him*. Matthew 22:37-40, John 14:15. But your enemy, Satan, is pushing you opposite; he's making you angry, proud, defensive, frustrated, afraid, anxious, depressed. He's dividing a friendship, telling you God's not listening, distracting you from your quiet time with busyness.... Sound familiar?

Your enemy is a prowling lion, looking for the first chance to pounce on you and devour you. 1 Peter 5:8. *But that doesn't mean you need to be afraid of him.*

Because **Satan is not all-powerful.** In fact, **you have a Power within you far greater — Love.** 1 John 4:18. Love is opposite everything Satan stands for. Because **God is Love.**

When you stand in Love, Satan loses. Every time.

No matter how things look to you, or whether everything turns out the way you expect it to or not, *you are more than a conqueror through Love.* Romans 8:31-39.

When you choose God as your Protector, *"you will tread on the lion and the cobra; you will trample the great lion and the serpent."* Psalm 91:13.

1 Cor. 13
- ☐ lacking in love
- ☐ taking pride in my spiritual gifts
- ☐ using my gifts without love
- ☐ looking down on those who don't speak in tongues
- ☐ looking down on those who don't have my gift
- ☐ giving someone a "word from God" in a hurtful way
- ☐ showing off my faith without love
- ☐ false gift of helps

> Ask the Lord how He wants you to trample Satan's schemes with love this week. Write in your journal what He shows you, and step out in obedience. John 14:15. Then journal your experience.

5 Victory Strategy
Know the Truth

John 8:31-32, 42-47; 10:10; 14:6, 15-17; 16:13

1 Cor. 13 ...

- ☐ giving to or helping others from motives other than love (like guilt, obligation, seeking acceptance, recognition, approval, _____, _____, _____, _____)
- ☐ martyr complex
- ☐ allowing harm to come to myself for motives other than love (like to gain attention, to "punish" someone who didn't love me the way I wanted, to show how righteous I am, _____, _____)
- ☐ false burden-bearing
- ☐ false guilt
- ☐ false responsibility
- ☐ _____
  _____

Satan comes to steal, kill, and destroy. But Christ came to give you abundant life. John 10:10.

Everything good and holy that Jesus stands for, Satan is the opposite. But *if you don't know your King well enough to distinguish the counterfeit, you could fall prey to Satan's deception*, just like the religious leaders in the New Testament did. John 8:42-47. They thought they were on God's side when they hung Jesus on the cross.

It's easy to look at their sin, and think, "I'd never do that." Maybe. Maybe not. If you were Eve, would you have eaten that fruit? All of us have sinned and fallen short of the glory of God. Romans 3:23. And you can be sure that *behind every sin you or anyone else has ever committed are* **enemy lies** *that led you there*.

The good news is Jesus doesn't just *speak* truth, He *is* Truth. John 8:31-32; 14:6. And **Truth topples lies to set the sinner free.**

To distinguish true currency from false, bankers don't study the counterfeit, they get to know the real deal. In the same way, the best way to recognize when the enemy's throwing you a lie is to walk so closely to Truth that any step outside the movement of His Spirit feels so wrong, so uncomfortable, you immediately click back in step. Galatians 5:25. (See the Galatians Gauge in Strategy 13.)

Throughout this book, we will look at strategies to recognize Satan's deceptions and triumph over him through the power of the One Whose name is Truth and Love.

> ASK THE LORD TO SHOW YOU ANY WRONG THOUGHT PROCESSES OR OTHER WAYS THE ENEMY HAS DECEIVED YOU INTO THINKING AND DOING WHAT HE WANTS INSTEAD OF OBEYING THE SPIRIT OF TRUTH. JOHN 14:15-17, 16:13; GALATIANS 5:22-25. JOURNAL YOUR THOUGHTS AND ASK JESUS FOR HIS TRUTH. WRITE WHAT HE SHOWS YOU.

Let Jesus take the lead

Victory Strategy 6

Galatians 5:22-25; Hebrews 10:14; John 14:1-3

If you've been dancing to Satan's tune in certain areas of your life since childhood, you may need to learn some new steps. And unlearning old habits isn't easy.

But once you get the hang of grabbing Jesus' hand and letting Him take the lead, it's all a glorious Cinderella story from here on out!

He calls you beautiful, *perfect*, because that is who you are in Him. Song of Songs 4:7, Hebrews 10:14. If you're willing, He will trample your old lie slave master, take you in His arms, and dance you all the way to that castle He's prepared for you in glory. John 14:1-3, Revelation 7:15-17.

It's not a fairy tale. This love beyond measure is what you were created for. And as perfect as it will be in Heaven, His love is no less glorious here on earth.

In fact, this is your time right now to get to know Him as Savior, Healer, Rescuer, Protector, and all His beautiful names, because once you get to Heaven, there will be no more war, illness, or evil for Him to rescue you from.

So, grab His hand, let Him take the lead, and waltz into oneness with Him.

This is where Heaven meets earth. Right now in your trying life and difficult circumstances. Right here in His loving, powerful arms.

1 Cor. 13 ...
- ☐ self-importance
- ☐ self-righteousness
- ☐ impatience
- ☐ unreasonable expectations
- ☐ easily agitated or upset
- ☐ cross
- ☐ snapping at others
- ☐ thoughtless
- ☐ pushy
- ☐ driving self
- ☐ driving others
- ☐ nagging
- ☐ forcing
- ☐ self-ambitious
- ☐ trampling or hurting others to get ahead or reach a goal

> CLOSE YOUR EYES. ASK THE LORD TO SHOW YOU A PICTURE OF YOU DANCING WITH HIM. ARE THERE NEW STEPS YOU NEED TO LEARN? OLD ONES YOU NEED TO STOP DOING? LET HIM DRAW YOU NEAR AND TEACH YOU STEP BY STEP HOW TO GO THROUGH LIFE AND TRIALS AS ONE WITH HIM.

7 Victory Strategy

Wear your armor

Ephesians 6:10-18, Romans 13:14, 2 Corinthians 5:3

1 Cor. 13 ...

- ☐ unmerciful
- ☐ unfair
- ☐ without pity
- ☐ unkind
- ☐ speaking hurtful or needless words
- ☐ irritable
- ☐ touchy
- ☐ intolerant
- ☐ unreasonable
- ☐ irrational
- ☐ careless
- ☐ impulsive
- ☐ lacking self-control
- ☐ reckless
- ☐ uncaring
- ☐ selfish
- ☐ unconcerned for others' welfare
- ☐ apathetic
- ☐ saying cutting remarks
- ☐ speaking or acting in a mean way toward
  - ☐ spouse
  - ☐ children
  - ☐ parents
  - ☐ authority
- ☐ _____
- ☐ _____
- ☐ _____
- ☐ _____

A friend of mine overheard two mediums talking at a New Age convention, assessing which Christians there to share Christ were a threat and which were not. "That's a Christian over there," one of them said to the other. "You can tell by his armor. Stay clear of him. But this one over here's dropped his. It's all clumped up around his feet."

In the spiritual realm, our armor is real, and the enemy can see quite clearly when you've dropped yours.

In the list below from Ephesians 6:14-17, note the capitalized words for each piece of spiritual armor. *Those are names of God.* HE is your Protector, your Shield, your Defender. Let Him cover you completely, so you will not be found naked when you're up against the enemy. Romans 13:14, 2 Corinthians 5:3, Ephesians 6:10-20.

The belt of TRUTH guards you from being tripped up by enemy lies.

The breastplate of RIGHTEOUSNESS guards your heart.

The readiness that comes from the gospel of PEACE protects your feet as you march into battle.

The SHIELD of faith covers you such that enemy arrows bounce off and even hit the one trying to hit you!

The helmet of SALVATION protects your mind from enemy assaults.

The sword of the Spirit, the WORD of God, slices through every lie and deception.

And *prayer is what keeps you walking as one with your King, so when He moves you're right there with Him.* Ephesians 6:18.

> WALK THROUGH EPHESIANS 6:10-18 WITH THE LORD TODAY IN PRAYER, CONSCIOUSLY PUTTING ON EACH PIECE OF ARMOR, AND RECOGNIZING THAT HE COVERS YOU.

Know the targets to demolish

Victory Strategy 8

2 Corinthians 10:3-5

> "For though we live in the world, we do not wage war as the world does. The weapons we fight with are not the weapons of the world. On the contrary, they have **divine power** to **demolish strongholds**. We **demolish arguments and every pretension that sets itself up against the knowledge of God**, and we **take captive every thought** to **make it obedient to Christ**."

2 Corinthians 10:3-5 describes our weapons, marks our targets, and maps our path to victory.

First, we don't battle with weapons of words, fists, or guns, like the world does. Rather, the power in our heavenly weapons is not of this world. It comes from God. It's ***divine***.

Second, we're not tearing down people or earthly structures, but Satanic strongholds built by arguments that set themselves up against the knowledge of God; in other words, ***lies*** contrary to Truth.

The way we demolish these wrong thought processes that control our mindsets and actions is to **hand our thoughts over to Jesus until they bow to what He says.**

According to Jesus, those thoughts are equal to the actions themselves. Matthew 5:28.

TAKE A LOOK AGAIN AT WHAT YOU'VE MARKED SO FAR IN THE RUNNING LIST ON THE SIDES. WHICH OF THOSE ARE WRONG THOUGHT PROCESSES? HOW DO THOSE THOUGHTS DRAW YOU AWAY FROM GOD AND INTO SIN? HOW WILL YOU LET LOVE AND TRUTH TEAR THEM DOWN? JOURNAL YOUR ANSWERS.

---

1 Cor. 13 cont.

- ☐ emotionally abusive
- ☐ verbally abusive
- ☐ sexually abusive
- ☐ physically abusive
- ☐ hitting my children in anger
- ☐ telling my children "no" just because I want to, not because it's something wrong
- ☐ often rejecting my husband's advances
- ☐ denying my husband sex
- ☐ provoking my children to anger

9 Victory Strategy

Remove the barriers

Psalm 32; John 8:31-32; 14:15-21; Matthew 17:20

1 Cor. 13 ...

- ☐ doing something just because I can, not because it's loving
- ☐ attacking
- ☐ thinking or assuming evil of others
- ☐ relying on my negative feelings or assumptions of others rather than seeking the truth
- ☐ wishing I had what someone else does
- ☐ comparison
- ☐ competition
- ☐ feeling that others are being unfair to me
- ☐ pouting
- ☐ withdrawing from those God has called me to love
- ☐ reclusive
- ☐ ignoring
- ☐ not listening
- ☐ letting my thoughts distract me from loving others

Through negative life experiences and wrong thought processes, the enemy has embedded lies, sins, and self-protective habits (strongholds) so deeply in your heart that **your will alone is not enough to break free.**

You need Someone stronger.

If you still don't know what I'm talking about, don't worry. I was there, too. My wrong thought processes were so habitual they felt "normal," not shameful or dirty like sin should feel. That's why I couldn't find them. Well, some of them, anyway. Others were *blaringly loud*.

But then ... *Jesus* ... He slipped into my quiet times and gently tapped at the walls in my heart, saying, "Open up. Let Me show you what's in here taking up space where I want to be."

You see, the mess within me had piled so high, it rose like a mountain between us, blocking His voice and side-tracking me from the *oneness* I was created for in Him.

Sin and the wrong thought processes that lead us there are the greatest barriers to hearing God's voice and experiencing the fullness of His love.

Each time He set me free from one of my old habits, I could hear His voice clearer, obey Him easier, and experience more of His power flowing through me.

Can you see how the enemy tries to deter us from oneness with Christ? I'm still on a journey, and will be until this life is over and I see Jesus face to face. But now I know, *mountains do come down.*

WHAT BARRIERS STAND BETWEEN YOU AND GOD? WRITE A PRAYER, INVITING HIM TO REMOVE THOSE, AND ASKING HIM TO MAKE YOU A CLEAR CHANNEL FOR HIS POWERFUL LOVE TO FLOW THROUGH TO OTHERS.

CONTINUE EACH DAY THROUGH THE CHECKLIST, ASKING GOD TO REVEAL TO YOU ANYTHING THAT BLOCKS YOU FROM MORE OF HIM. REPENT, USE THE TRUTH ENCOUNTER IN STRATEGY 18 AS YOU NEED TO, AND WRITE YOUR PRAYERS, EXPERIENCES, AND WHAT GOD IS SAYING TO YOU IN YOUR JOURNAL.

The James 4 Principle

Ephesians 2:8; James 4:7-8; Romans 8:28

Victory Strategy 10

Every strategy in this book is nestled in this principle:

To overcome the enemy, *draw near to God*. James 4:7-8.
1. Invite God near by **drawing near to Him** yourself.
2. Let God help you **clear away whatever blocks you** from hearing Him and feeling His touch.
3. Say **no to the enemy**'s plans for your life.

In other words, **resist the enemy. Pursue God.**

It sounds simpler than it is, of course. But once you start practicing winning strategies for drawing near to God, and those become new habits built into your lifestyle, *the joy, freedom, and thrill of God's felt presence will be so intoxicating,* **He will be all you want**, *and those old temptations the enemy once used to win you over to his side will lose their appeal.*

Flee the enemy, and he will flee from you. Pursue God, and you will find Him right here with you.

> MEMORIZE JAMES 4:7-8. WHAT STEPS CAN YOU TAKE TO ACTIVELY FLEE THE ENEMY AND PURSUE GOD TODAY? ASK GOD, AND WRITE THE PLANS AND INSTRUCTIONS HE SHOWS YOU IN YOUR JOURNAL.

1 Cor. 13 ...
- ☐ too busy forming my argument to listen
- ☐ looking at my phone, watch, device, or something else while someone is talking to me
- ☐ leaving the room (or wishing I could) instead of listening when someone's talking
- ☐ dismissing others' sorrow
- ☐ bored with others' conversation
- ☐ lack of compassion

11 Victory Strategy

Live Kingdom Culture

Romans 8; 12:2; 1 Peter 2:11-12; John 16:33; Psalm 45:10-11

1 Cor. 13 …

- ☐ letting electronics or worldly matters keep me from quality time with others
- ☐ prioritizing my own ambition, work, selfish desires, etc., over being there for others, especially my family
- ☐ subjective (my point of view is the best or right or only one)
- ☐ self-absorbed
- ☐ picky
- ☐ burdensome
- ☐ boastful
- ☐ concerned with self-gratification
- ☐ self-indulgent
- ☐ self-aware (thinking constantly about how I look or how others see me or what I think about myself)

When you chose to follow Christ, you became a daughter of the Most High God, heir to His Kingdom alongside His Son Jesus. Your loyalties changed, and so did your home. Now you are an "alien," a stranger just passing through this earth.

Your home is Heaven and your loyalties are to your Father and King. Your culture is no longer the one you grew up in or live in; it is **Kingdom Culture**.

That means, **you no longer do things the way others expect you to or the way the enemy wants you to. *You follow your King. You do what Jesus does.***

That isn't always easy. There are battles of our flesh, our desire to please others, our habits and traditions, our will, and other, even fiercer enemies that fight against our desire to walk as one with Christ.

To know how Kingdom Culture calls you to act and react, you must not only ***know the Truth***, but ***live it***. (See Strategies 24-28.)

> SPEND SOME TIME WITH THE LORD TODAY LOOKING AT THE PIECES OF THE CULTURE YOU LIVE IN OR GREW UP IN THAT YOU HAVE INCORPORATED INTO YOUR THOUGHTS AND ACTIONS, BUT THAT DO NOT LINE UP WITH KINGDOM CULTURE.
>
> THEN ASK JESUS HOW HE WOULD DO THAT. WRITE IN YOUR JOURNAL WHAT HE SHOWS YOU, AND BEGIN WALKING OUT IN THAT KINGDOM CULTURE OPPOSITE.

The Three-Fold Sieve

Victory Strategy 12

John 8:42-47; 10:1-5, 27

God speaks in many ways. Just a few the Bible mentions are the Word (2 Timothy 3:16-17), circumstances (2 Corinthians 12:7-10; Psalm 40:1-3), others (1 Corinthians 2:4-13), His still small voice in your mind and heart (Psalm 42:8), **dreams and visions** (Acts 2:17), **impressions** or **urgings** (Acts 15:28), a sense of **peace** (Philippians 4:7), **nature** (Psalm 125; 19:1-4), signs and wonders (Acts 2:17-21), etc.

For each of these and more, the enemy has counterfeits. He twists Scripture, brings traumatic events into your life to paint lies on your heart, delivers false prophecies, dreams or nightmares, and even performs false miracles.

How will you distinguish God's voice from the enemy's?

THREE-FOLD SIEVE FOR DISCERNING GOD'S VOICE OF TRUTH:

1. Does it **line up with God's Word**—not just one portion, but *all of it? The Word must be interpreted by the Word.* If your interpretation of a verse or passage does not agree with the rest of the Bible, then there's something wrong with your interpretation, not the Word.
2. Does it **line up with God's character**—*especially His love and grace?* 1 John 4:16, Matthew 22:37-40.
3. Does it **draw you (and others) closer to Him**?

1 Cor. 13 ...
- ☐ *insisting on having my own way*
- ☐ *desire for attention or recognition*
- ☐ *feeling I know more than others*
- ☐ *looking down on those who don't share my viewpoint*
- ☐ *self-exalting*
- ☐ *justifying my faults; self-justification*
- ☐ *self-seeking*
- ☐ *closed-minded*
- ☐ *stubborn*
- ☐ *rude*
- ☐ *over-indulgent*

> RUN SOME OF YOUR THOUGHTS FROM YOUR DAY TODAY THROUGH THE THREE-FOLD SIEVE. WRITE IN YOUR JOURNAL HOW THEY AGREE OR DISAGREE.
>
> GET IN THE HABIT OF TAKING YOUR THOUGHTS CAPTIVE THROUGHOUT THE DAY EVERY DAY USING THE THREE-FOLD SIEVE. 2 CORINTHIANS 10:5.

13 Victory Strategy

The Galatians Gauge
Galatians 5:22-25

1 Cor. 13 ...

- ☐ closing myself off from others
- ☐ easily angered
- ☐ belligerent
- ☐ contentious
- ☐ confrontational
- ☐ aggressive
- ☐ overly sensitive
- ☐ emotionally unstable
- ☐ flying off the handle (tirades)
- ☐ easily hurt
- ☐ letting grief so overtake me that I no longer reach out to others
- ☐ keeping a record of wrongs
- ☐ unforgiving
- ☐ not responding to those who ask forgiveness
- ☐ not asking forgiveness when I've hurt others
- ☐ blaming others for my problems
- ☐ _____
- ☐ _____

When you dance in step with the Spirit (Galatians 5:25), He is the One leading your thoughts and reactions.

So, one quick way to notice whenever you're under "enemy attack" is to check for negative thoughts, feelings, or reactions outside of the fruit of the Spirit.

LIST AND MEMORIZE THE FRUIT IN GALATIANS 5:22-23:

_____ _____
_____ _____
_____ _____
_____

WHEN WAS THE LAST TIME YOU FELT ANGRY, FRUSTRATED, DEPRESSED, JEALOUS, OR REACTED IN SOME OTHER NEGATIVE WAY OUTSIDE THE FRUIT OF THE SPIRIT? WHAT WERE YOU THINKING WHEN YOU REACTED THAT WAY? ASK GOD TO SHOW YOU.

NOW, RUN THOSE THOUGHTS THROUGH THE

THREE-FOLD SIEVE:

1. LORD, HOW DOES THAT REACTION/THOUGHT DISAGREE WITH WHAT YOU SAY IN YOUR WORD?
2. HOW DOES IT DISAGREE WITH YOUR LOVE AND GRACE?
3. HOW DOES IT DRAW ME AND/OR OTHERS AWAY FROM YOU?

WRITE WHAT GOD SHOWS YOU IN YOUR JOURNAL.

Follow the feelings to the lies

John 8:31-32; 42-47; 14:15-18; 2 Corinthians 4:7

Victory Strategy 14

What you feel is directly related to what you believe.

So, if you feel something negative outside the fruit of the Spirit, like impatience, boredom, jealousy, etc., get alone with the Lord as soon as you can and ask Him where that comes from. *When was the first time that feeling or attitude entered your heart?* Ask Him.

Lies are pressed into our hearts through experience.

So, *ask God to take you to a memory He wants to heal.* You need to see and understand where the feelings come from so you can find the lies and let God set you free.

A lie is anything contrary to what God says. For example, if you believe, "I'm a failure," "I'm stupid," or "I can't do anything right," no matter how "true" those statements feel, they are contrary to Philippians 4:13, 1 Corinthians 1:20-29, and God's character of grace.

Lies also have a **wrong focus**. Do you see the word "I" repeated over and over in the above paragraph? **The fruit of the Spirit will fade fast in you if your eyes ("I"s) are on your own ability rather than the all-surpassing greatness of the Sovereign One Who loves you and lives within you.**

1 Cor. 13 ...
- ☐ delighting in evil
- ☐ delighting in others' struggles
- ☐ self-protective
- ☐ hopeless
- ☐ wanting harm to come to those who have done harm to me
- ☐ treating others with contempt or hard feelings
- ☐ blocking others out
- ☐ keeping my distance
- ☐ not building deep friendships
- ☐ _____
- ☐ _____

> Ask Jesus, "What are You telling me that I'm not believing?" Write in your journal what He shows you, and then ask Him to help you believe.
>
> As God shows you lies in your thought processes, write those on the left in your journal (Page 32 in *Delight to Be a Woman of Wonder Prayer Journal*, or see example below.) Then ask Him for His truth, and write that to the right. Don't worry if you don't hear God straight away. Just leave it blank until He walks you through experiences or encounters (Strategy 18) to reveal His truth.

LIES	TRUTH
I'm stupid.	Worldly wisdom isn't worth boasting in. The only One who is truly wise lives within me. My boast is in Him. Not my own intellect. 1 Cor. 1:20-31. He has made me perfect. Hebrews 10:14.

15 Victory Strategy

Recognize strongholds

Romans 7:15-21; 2 Corinthians 10:3-5; John 8:42-47

1 Cor. 13 ...
- ☐ choosing lies over truth
- ☐ not rejoicing with the truth
- ☐ not protecting others
- ☐ reacting defensively to others' remarks
- ☐ distrustful
- ☐ suspicious
- ☐ withdrawn
- ☐ avoiding those God has called me to love
- ☐ giving others a cold shoulder
- ☐ loss of heart
- ☐ nothing to look forward to
- ☐ despair
- ☐ breaking promises
- ☐ disapproving of others
- ☐ disappointed in others
- ☐ not seeking reconciliation
- ☐ giving up on a relationship with a family member or friend, not trying anymore

Do you feel sometimes like certain sins or thought patterns have a strong hold on you? Like you know what you should be thinking or doing, but you end up doing the opposite anyway?

A stronghold is a thought process or sin habit contrary to Kingdom Culture that motivates or controls you in that area of your life rather than the Holy Spirit.

The building blocks of strongholds are lies, or "arguments against the knowledge of God." 2 Corinthians 10:3-5. The stronger the lie, the firmer the walls of your prison. *Those lies must come down for you to be free.*

For example, if your parents praised your siblings but not you as you were growing up, you might feel, "I don't measure up." The enemy could then confirm that lie through other negative experiences, like a bad test grade, rejection from a boyfriend, losing a job, etc. He might even add a few more lies, like, "I'm not good enough," "I'm not pretty enough," "I'll never have that," or "Why do I even try?" Those thoughts become the building blocks for strongholds like defeat, rejection, low self-esteem, etc., making you feel depressed, unfulfilled, unworthy....

> IN WHAT AREAS OF YOUR LIFE HAS THE ENEMY TAKEN YOU CAPTIVE TO DO HIS WILL? ASK GOD TO SHOW YOU THE STRONGHOLDS HE WANTS TO BRING DOWN, AND THEN USE THE TRUTH ENCOUNTER STEPS IN STRATEGY 18 TO POSITION YOURSELF FOR FREEDOM.

Remove guardian lies
Psalm 142:7; Isaiah 42:18-22; Matthew 18:15

Victory Strategy 16

Most strongholds feel so "normal" we don't even realize they're there.

That's because the enemy likes to **guard** them with excuses:
- "That's just the way I am."
- "This is just the way God made me."
- "Everyone struggles with that."
- "I'm not so bad."
- "I'm not hurting anyone, so what does it matter?"
- "I need this."
- "I can't help it."
- "I guess this is just the cross I have to bear."
- "I'll never be free."

There is no stronghold more powerful than Jesus. To believe anything else is just ridiculous! **Jesus is standing right here right now, poised to set you free.** *Let Him!*

> WHICH OF THOSE GUARDIAN LIES ABOVE HAVE YOU THOUGHT BEFORE? WHAT THOUGHT PROCESSES, ACTIONS, OR LACK OF ACTION WERE THEY PROTECTING? WERE THERE OTHER LIES GUARDING THAT, TOO? ASK GOD, AND WRITE IN YOUR JOURNAL WHAT HE SHOWS YOU.
>
> EVEN IF YOU CAN'T SEE YOUR STRONGHOLDS, THEY ARE SELDOM HIDDEN FROM THOSE AROUND YOU. HAS ANYONE EVER TRIED TO TALK TO YOU ABOUT YOUR ISSUES OR ACTIONS THAT HURT OTHERS, BUT YOU RESPONDED IN SELF-DEFENSE, BLAME, OR SOME OTHER WAY BESIDES LISTENING AND REPENTANCE? ASK GOD, AND WRITE IN YOUR JOURNAL WHAT HE SHOWS YOU.

Don't play the blame game. *The best way to miss what God is showing you is to point a finger at someone else.*

1 Cor. 13 ...
- ☐ *focusing on how the other person needs to change, rather than letting God change me*
- ☐ *not cleaning up the messes I cause in others' lives*
- ☐ *negative*
- ☐ *unfaithful*
- ☐ *untrustworthy*
- ☐ *not being there for someone in hard times*
- ☐ *unwilling to help, especially for selfish reasons*
- ☐ _____
- ☐ _____

17 Victory Strategy: Scrub off the whitewash

Ezekiel 13:10-16; Matthew 22:37-40; 1 Corinthians 16:14

1 Cor. 13 ...

- ☐ putting myself above others
- ☐ unwilling to love
- ☐ unwilling to receive love
- ☐ know-it-all
- ☐ acting childish
- ☐ childish reasoning
- ☐ not persevering in faith
- ☐ straying off-course from God's road
- ☐ trusting in my abilities over God's
- ☐ not trusting God for the outcome
- ☐ not trusting in God's Sovereignty
- ☐ defeatist attitude
- ☐ not hoping in God
- ☐ choosing anything else as a priority over love
- ☐ unable to receive love
- ☐ _____
- ☐ _____
- ☐ _____

Sometimes we don't recognize our own strongholds because the lie-walls are covered with **whitewash**, like

- "I'm not judging. I'm just telling it like it is."
- "Well, she really should...."
- "He deserved it."
- "I don't mean to talk behind her back, but ..., so you'll pray for her, of course."
- "I'm right. You're wrong."
- "The Bible says...."

The point of whitewash is to paint your sin so pretty you overlook it. Satan, our deceiver, loves to make us feel "righteous" when we agree with him, so we'll think we're doing something "good" or "right" — *even that we're agreeing with God.*

Such camouflage is especially useful in hiding strongholds like a religious spirit, spiritual pride, judgment, legalism, accusation, self-righteousness, persecution, slander, gossip, pride, etc.

To tell the difference between what God's doing and what Satan's using you to do, ***don't rely on self-righteous excuses.*** Run your thoughts through the Three-Fold Sieve:

1. Does it agree with **ALL of God's Word**, not just the part you're standing on to beat people over the head?
2. Are you being **loving**? Humble? Is that what grace would do?
3. Are your actions **drawing others in** to God, or pushing them away? How?

You can also look at your attitude or feeling, and **check it with the Galatians Gauge**. Is love, peace, kindness, self-control, etc., motivating your thoughts and actions, or is jealousy, pride, self-righteousness, etc., motivating you?

> ASK THE LORD TO SHOW YOU ANY WAYS YOUR SIN MAY BE WHITEWASHED. USE THE METHODS ABOVE TO SCRUB THE WALLS, THEN REPENT AND SEEK GOD IN A TRUTH ENCOUNTER (STRATEGY 18), IF HE LEADS. WRITE YOUR EXPERIENCE IN YOUR JOURNAL.

Truth Encounter

Victory Strategy 18

John 14:6; Isaiah 55:6-9; Psalm 51:6; 107:20

Only a deep, personal encounter with Truth Himself can topple the lie-walls that build anger, depression, judgment, fear, or any other stronghold you're captive to.

Truth Encounter steps to freedom:

1. Ask God to guard this time together with Him, to fill the room with His presence, block out any distractions or enemy interference, and lead you.
2. Ask Him, *"When did (rejection, lust, loneliness, impatience, anger, judgment, or whatever your issue is) first enter my life? Take me anywhere You want to take me and show me anything You want to show me."*
3. If a memory comes to mind, stay there with Him, feeling what you felt when that happened. Look for the lies (like, *"I'll never measure up," "I have to do this on my own," "No one will ever love me,"* etc.).
4. Now, ask Him for His truth: *"Lord, You were there when that happened. Show me where You were and what You were saying and doing. What do You say to the lies and to what happened to me?"*
5. Look around for Him in your memory, and listen for His still small voice, a Bible verse, a picture, an impression of His love and truth upon your heart and mind. *He may even change the memory to reflect what He says and what He was doing.*

1 Samuel 15:22; John 14:15

- ☐ going through the motions of church or serving God without true love for Him or desire to obey
- ☐ disobeying God
- ☐ compartmentalizing: God is for Sunday and Bible study; the rest of the time I do things my way
- ☐ having the appearance of devotion to God without true surrender
- ☐ _____

WHAT RECURRING REACTIONS OR THOUGHT PROCESSES HAVE BEEN PULLING YOU DOWN LATELY?

WALK THROUGH THESE STEPS ABOVE TOGETHER WITH THE LORD AND LET HIS TRUTH SET YOU FREE.

WHAT WERE THE LIES YOU BELIEVED?

WHAT IS HIS TRUTH? RUN THAT THROUGH THE THREE-FOLD SIEVE (STRATEGY 12).

WRITE YOUR EXPERIENCE IN YOUR JOURNAL.

19 Victory Strategy: Picture freedom. Stay free.

Romans 7:15-25; Galatians 5:1, 25

James 1:2-8
- ☐ depression
- ☐ frustration
- ☐ disappointment
- ☐ discouragement
- ☐ feeling annoyed
- ☐ giving up
- ☐ not persevering under trials
- ☐ unwise
- ☐ leaning on my own "wisdom" rather than God's
- ☐ doubting God
- ☐ wavering in faith
- ☐ tossed about by storms of life
- ☐ double-minded
- ☐ unstable
- ☐ undependable

Isaiah 30:15
- ☐ unrepentant
- ☐ agitated
- ☐ restless
- ☐ not resting in God
- ☐ _____
- ☐ _____
- ☐ _____

It's helpful to have a picture before you of what freedom from your strongholds will look like. Not only will that motivate you to press on for truth, but you'll be able to recognize freedom when you get there.

And *stay on path*.

Because dogs return to lap up what they just vomited, as Proverbs 26:11 and 2 Peter 2:22 so graphically put it. And newly washed pigs just go right back to wallowing in stinky, sloshy, feces and mud.

So, there you have two clear, biblical pictures of where you *don't* want to go when Jesus sets you free.

But let me wave at you the sweet fragrance of what freedom has been like for me. When I was a slave to my strongholds, it was if they controlled me from the inside, like they were a part of me I couldn't get rid of. I'd "repent" so many times, but just find myself back in that same old negative reaction or sin all over again.

Once Truth set me free, however, the temptations and lies felt more as if they came from the *outside*.

As if I had a *choice*.

As if I could just put up my shield and knock those lies down. In fact, now that I know the truth, so many of *those old lies sound so silly I even laugh*.

In other words, now I can **choose to walk in the Spirit**.

In fact, **the more I walk in Truth and obedience, the weaker the lies, until they eventually disappear altogether.**

Now, that's *sweet!*

ASK THE LORD FOR A PICTURE OF WHAT FREEDOM FROM EACH STRONGHOLD WILL LOOK LIKE FOR YOU. WRITE WHAT HE SHOWS YOU IN YOUR JOURNAL.

HOW BADLY DO YOU WANT THAT? BECAUSE, FOR MOST OF MY STRONGHOLDS, I HAD TO WANT FREEDOM BADLY ENOUGH TO LEAVE MY PRISON FOREVER WHEN JESUS BLASTED THE LIE-WALLS DOWN.

Repulsed by your sin
Psalm 32; 66:18; 143:10

Victory Strategy 20

Are you motivated now, after picturing freedom versus captivity in Strategy 19? Want some more dynamite to set around your stronghold?

Ask God how He sees your sin.

He may show you how it grieves Him, or affects those you sin against, or separates you from Him, blocking you from the breathtaking wonders He has prepared for you.

So, sit there, staring at what He shows you, until you **hate** how your sin affects those you love, until you're **so repulsed you never want to go back there again**.

That's what happened with my pride. God and I had been chipping away at the lie-bricks and rebuilding my heart-temple with truth-stones for a year. Then one night, He pointed His loving, holy finger at all the times He had brought people into my path for me to share the Good News with, but I didn't, because *I was afraid of what they'd think of me*.

How sick is that? Throwing away someone's chance at eternity because of my own selfishness, fear and pride! If Christ loved them so much He *died* for them, the least I can do is *tell* them.

That was that! I hated my pride so much I never wanted to go there again. The walls came down and I ended up in a surrendered heap on the floor at God's feet.

I'll never be the same again. I'm still human, of course, and I still need to keep a guard up against pride, but now I can see it more clearly. I can choose not to bow to it; whereas before, pride most often controlled me.

Philippians 3:19; 1 Corinthians 10:23

- [ ] bowing to the god of the stomach
- [ ] gluttony
- [ ] bulimia
- [ ] anorexia
- [ ] fixation on food
- [ ] obeying my own desires rather than following the Spirit's leading
- [ ] eating when I'm not hungry
- [ ] overeating
- [ ] not taking good care of my body as God's temple
- [ ] not having a healthy diet
- [ ] _____

> ASK GOD TO SHOW YOU HOW HE SEES YOUR SIN. HOW DOES IT AFFECT THE PEOPLE AROUND YOU? HOW DOES IT HURT GOD'S HEART?
>
> WRITE WHAT HE SHOWS YOU IN YOUR JOURNAL. HATE YOUR SIN SO MUCH YOU NEVER GO BACK THERE AGAIN!

21 Victory Strategy

Refill the empty places
Luke 11:24-26; Jeremiah 31:28; Ephesians 4:28

Luke 10:38-42

- [ ] focus on works more than relationship
- [ ] busyness
- [ ] perfectionism
- [ ] distractedness
- [ ] looking down on those who don't work as hard as I think I do
- [ ] prioritizing other things over time with God
- [ ] jealousy of those close to Jesus
- [ ] judging others for not sharing my priorities
- [ ] focusing on sin I perceive in others, but ignoring my own sin
- [ ] asking God to change others when I'm the problem
- [ ] worried
- [ ] upset
- [ ] missing out on what matters most

In order to walk out in the fullness of freedom, and not return to those old habits of thinking and reacting, you will need God's help to make **lifestyle changes that block the enemy out**. Galatians 5:1.

Begin with asking the Lord to **refill you with the opposite Kingdom Culture quality** — to replace the "empty space" where that anger, lust, or frustration was before with *Himself*.

1 John 4:18 is a perfect example of this. When your heart is filled up and overflowing with love, fear can't reside there, because there's no room for it. Love pushes it out.

> WHAT IS THE KINGDOM CULTURE OPPOSITE OF A STRONGHOLD GOD IS SETTING YOU FREE FROM NOW? ASK HIM TO REPLACE ANGER WITH GRACE, IMPATIENCE WITH PATIENCE, FEAR WITH FAITH AND LOVE, ETC.
>
> WHAT NEW HABITS OR LIFESTYLE CHANGES IS HE CALLING YOU TO? WHAT SPECIAL INSTRUCTIONS IS HE GIVING YOU, ESPECIALLY IN THE FACE OF CIRCUMSTANCES OR PEOPLE THAT NORMALLY TRIGGER THOSE OLD REACTIONS? ASK HIM, AND SEEK HIM FOR A PLAN TO LIVE IN FREEDOM.
>
> DON'T EXPECT TO GET EVERYTHING JUST RIGHT AT FIRST. YOU HAVE TO "EXERCISE" THOSE SPIRITUAL MUSCLES IN ORDER TO BUILD UP STRENGTH AND RUN WELL. JUST KEEP YOUR EYES FIXED ON THE PRIZE, YOUR KING, AND DON'T STOP RUNNING TOWARD HIM.
>
> EXPECT THE LORD TO ALLOW SPECIAL SITUATIONS AND CIRCUMSTANCES INTO YOUR LIFE NOW FOR YOU TO PRACTICE WHAT HE'S SHOWING YOU. ARE YOU FOLLOWING HIS INSTRUCTIONS IN THOSE CIRCUMSTANCES? IF NOT, WHAT DISTRACTS YOU?

Linked healing

Joshua 1:5; Psalm 107:20; 1 John 4:19

Victory strategy 22

Once you believe a lie, the enemy is likely to bring yet more experiences into your path to confirm it.

But **when Jesus sets you free,** whether through a Truth Encounter (Strategy 18) or some other way, **He often heals not only that first memory, but** *all the subsequent ones linked to that lie.*

Not that you forget what happened (although you just might; anything's possible with God), but **the negative response or feeling triggered by the memory should be gone**, and in many cases, *the memory itself transformed to see what Jesus was doing rather than what the enemy wanted you to receive.*

As a teenager, a close friend betrayed me, and the enemy planted in my tender heart, "No one will ever love me as much as I love them." Then he doubled his efforts over the next few years to confirm that lie through many abuses and betrayals by people I loved.

Finally, in a Truth Encounter, God took me back to that first memory. He said, "She couldn't love you with a mature love because she wasn't mature." Then He walked me through each of the other memories with other people, and that same truth had healed all of them!

At last, God pointed to my husband and said, "But *he* loves you with a mature love, because he *is* mature."

Now that Truth has set me free, I love others freely without worrying how much they love me back.

Revelation 3:1-6, 14-22
- ☐ apathy
- ☐ spiritual stagnancy
- ☐ complacency
- ☐ spiritual blindness
- ☐ stunted growth
- ☐ lack of passion for the things of God

1 Peter 2:1
- ☐ malice
- ☐ ill will
- ☐ deceit
- ☐ double-crossing
- ☐ hypocrisy
- ☐ envy
- ☐ slander
- ☐ _____
- ☐ _____

> ASK THE LORD TO SHOW YOU ANY MEMORIES LINKED TO A LIE HE HEALED YOU FROM IN A TRUTH ENCOUNTER IN STRATEGY 18. DO YOU NOTICE A DIFFERENCE NOW?
>
> WHAT DOES JESUS SAY ABOUT THOSE THINGS THAT HAPPENED TO YOU? HOW DOES THAT MAKE YOU FEEL? JOURNAL YOUR ANSWERS.

NOTE: *Some experiences are so complicated, they may take several Truth Encounters to heal completely. And in extreme trauma, like abuse or assault, it may be wise to seek a counselor or close friend you can trust to pray with you..*

23 Victory Strategy — Break unholy vows

Psalm 41:2; 91:14; 3:3; 5:12; 18:2,30; 28:7; 33:20; 84:11

Jonah 1:1-6

- ☐ *running from God*
- ☐ *doing the opposite of what God says*
- ☐ *disdain or lack of love for the lost*
- ☐ *not sharing God's love*
- ☐ *rebelling against God's call*
- ☐ *refusing to take a job or go where God leads*
- ☐ *not seeing others' needs or helping them*
- ☐ *not accepting responsibility for my sin*
- ☐ *rationalizing my sin*
- ☐ *letting others suffer the consequences of my sin*
- ☐ *distancing myself from those who suffer so I can do what I want in "peace"*
- ☐ *running from responsibility*

Have you ever gone through something so difficult you thought, "I'll never let that happen to me again," "I'll never do that again," or, "I'll ... if it's the last thing I do"?

Maybe you messed up, others mistreated you, or you fell for the wrong guy. But whatever your situation, *if you made a self-protective vow, you may have invited the enemy to deal you more than a few blows.*

Why? Because you aren't strong enough to protect yourself. Not by any means! **God is your Protector.** When you take over His job for Him, trading your true Shield for false protection, you leave yourself *exposed*. Your enemy is likely to seize the opportunity and attack you in that area of your life all the more.

Your words have power. Can you see how Satan might act on the vow, "I'll never give my heart to a man again"?

Satan can be a legalist, if it suits him; and if he feels your words give him the "right" or invitation to batter you, *he's likely to do just that!*

To break self-protective vows and step back under your holy Covering (John 14:20, Psalm 91), repent and pray something like, *"Lord, forgive me for making the vow, '_____.' I renounce and break that vow now in the name of Jesus, and I cancel any rights the enemy feels he has to pick on me because of it. I cut off any curses that may have fallen on me because of those words, and I release myself to live under Your protection, O Lord, for You alone are my Shield...."*

> HAVE YOU MADE ANY UNHOLY VOWS? ASK GOD.
>
> IN WHAT WAYS HAVE YOUR EFFORTS TO FULFILL THOSE VOWS RESULTED IN NEGATIVE OUTCOMES?
>
> SPEND TIME LISTENING TO THE LORD AND JOURNALING WHAT HE SHOWS YOU. THEN PRAY TO CANCEL THOSE VOWS AND INVITE GOD TO BE YOUR PROTECTOR.

One with your sword

Ephesians 6:17; Revelation 1:16

Victory Strategy 24

The Word of God is our foremost weapon against the enemy. What does Ephesians 6:17 call it?

_____

In Revelation 1:16, where does the Word come from?

_____

One great way to release the power of God into your prayers and defeat the enemy's purposes is to **pray back to the Lord what He has already said.**

When you pray the Word, you agree with God, and invite Him to fulfill His purposes and promises.

And that's *powerful*.

Each day in your quiet times, as you read the Word, try praying back to the Lord the passage you just read, especially the parts that touched you most.

You can also ask Him to give you verses to pray over each of the people on your prayer list. Convert those verses into a prayer, and write it in your journal. Then whenever you pray for them, start with that prayer and add whatever else God's leading you to pray for them.

> In light of the last strategy, practice praying the Word by inviting God to protect you and those in your care through Psalm 91.
>
> Write your prayer in your journal.
>
> It might look something like this: "I choose to dwell in Your shelter, O Most High, and rest in Your shadow, for You are Almighty. Pull me safely under Your wings. Be my Refuge and my Fortress, my God in Whom I trust. Save me from ..."

Hebrews 4:12

- [ ] *feeling conviction of sin when I read the Word, but then ignoring or forgetting*
- [ ] *not letting the Word change me*
- [ ] *not hungry for the Word*
- [ ] *bored of reading the Bible; feel like I've heard it all before*
- [ ] *not reading or studying the Bible regularly*
- [ ] *not believing the Bible relevant to my situation*
- [ ] _____

25 Victory Strategy

Handling your sword

Hebrews 4:12; Luke 4:1-13; Proverbs 3:5-8

Heb. 4:12 ...
- ☐ arguing against God's Word
- ☐ intellectual knowledge of the Word, without heart knowledge
- ☐ often feeling the urge to leave the room or fall asleep when the Bible is read
- ☐ not using the Word as my source for what I believe is true, right, and good
- ☐ not letting the Word penetrate my attitudes
- ☐ using the Word to cut or hurt others, or to block them from obeying Christ
- ☐ not training up others in the Word as I should, especially my children
- ☐ _____
- ☐ _____

In all things Kingdom Culture, Jesus is our Model. How did He use Scripture as a weapon against the enemy? Luke 4:4, 8, 12. _____
_____
_____

After the second time Jesus answered from God's Word, wily Satan threw in a bit of Scripture himself. Do you recognize the passage in verses 9-11?

Satan quoted Psalm 91 correctly, but **he twisted the meaning for purposes opposite God's.** We don't just go jump off a cliff because Satan tells us to and God said He'd protect us. We do what *God* wants us to do. We seek *Him* for His paths and follow *Him*, not Satan. Proverbs 3:5-8.

Don't use God's Word as an excuse to sin.

"Well," you might say, "I think Ephesians 4:26 says anger's not a sin if I get over it before I go to bed." How does that make it through the Three-Fold Sieve with verse 31 right on its tail, and other passages like Colossians 3:8, 1 Corinthians 13:5, James 1:19-20?

This is why it's so important for us to not just know certain portions of the Word. We need to know *all* of it. Because **we need to know GOD.**

Holy, loving God did not give us His Word to entice us to sin, enforce legalism, forbid a gender to talk about Him, look down on those who don't speak in tongues, or anything else contrary to the rest of Scripture and His heart of love and grace.

> GET IN THE HABIT OF READING, MEDITATING ON, AND STUDYING THE WORD. LOOK UP RELATED PASSAGES. DO WORD SEARCHES (STRATEGY 28) ON THE TOPICS THAT MOVE YOU. MEMORIZE THE VERSES GOD HIGHLIGHTS, SO, LIKE YOUR KING, YOU'LL BE READY TO USE YOUR SWORD IN THE FACE OF ENEMY ATTACKS.
>
> IS THERE ANY WAY YOU HAVE MISUSED SCRIPTURE FOR PURPOSES OPPOSITE LOVE? ASK GOD, AND WRITE WHAT HE SHOWS YOU IN YOUR JOURNAL.

Your sword's Name
Song of Songs 1:1; John 14:7

Victory strategy 26

Have you ever read the Bible and certain words or verses touched you deeply, right where you needed it most? That's a "kiss" of the Word. Song of Songs 1:2.

In John 1:1-5, 14, and Revelation 19:13, the Word has another name. What is it? _____

When you read God's Word, you are gazing at Jesus. He *is* the Word.

Do you want to see God? To know His heart, to feel His love, to touch Him? Then *open the Word*. He spent centuries putting His love letters into writing so you can know His heart. Why not spend a few minutes every day reading them?

Here's some trouble-shooting for your dry times: *****Study the Word together with the Lord in your morning quiet times**; but then at night, *****when you crawl into bed, open it again for a "goodnight kiss": r**ead until you feel His touch**, and fall asleep in His arms. *****Pray before you read the Bible, asking God to speak to your heart**. If you have trouble getting into a passage, *****ask the Lord if you're in the book He wants you to be** for this season. If not, read where You feel His touch. *****Underline the words that jump out at you**. *****Look up in a concordance** other passages with those words. Use your Bible like a journal and *****write in the margin what you feel God saying to your heart**, so each time you go back there, you get that kiss all over again. *****Ask others what God has taught them** through that passage. Pick a story about Jesus and *****ask Him which character you're most like in that story** and why. *****Close your eyes and ask God to show you a picture of that passage.** Where are you in that story? **Where is Jesus? What is He saying to you?** ....

The possibilities for drawing near are endless. So, don't give in to Satan's lie that the Word of God is boring. **There's nothing boring about Jesus!**

Galatians 1:6-10
☐ following traditions that don't agree with the Word
☐ standing on man's theologies rather than God's Word
☐ believing false teachings
☐ teaching from my own ideas rather than what the Word says
☐ confusion
☐ confusing others' faith
☐ choosing to obey man over God
☐ not obeying God's call to serve

> TRY ONE OR MORE OF THE SUGGESTIONS ABOVE* FOR HELPING YOU FALL IN LOVE WITH THE WORD, AND WRITE IN YOUR JOURNAL WHAT GOD SHOWS YOU.

27 Victory Strategy

Live by the sword
James 1:22-25; 2:14-20; 1 Corinthians 8:1b-3

2 Timothy 3:16

- ☐ teaching or preaching my own agenda, rather than the Word
- ☐ rebuking others based on my own opinions rather than the Word
- ☐ not teaching the Word or sharing with others what God is teaching me
- ☐ not leading, helping with, or participating in Bible study
- ☐ not teaching the Word to my children or others God leads me to
- ☐ not letting someone mentor me or help me grow spiritually that God has appointed to do so
- ☐ not mentoring others in the Word

It's not enough to know in your head what the Word says. It must make a difference in your life. It must *change* you.

Let the truth you know be the truth you live.

You may think you already do that, but there are still so many ways in which your earthly culture has formed you to do things opposite Kingdom Culture. What feels "right" or "righteous" to you may not actually be so in Heaven's eyes.

Whether you have a seminary degree or not, you can't let what you think, what you've been taught, what others say, or man's interpretations or theologies be the sand you stand on.

You must stand on the Rock, or you will fall. Matthew 7:24-27.

Know what your King says, and *do it*.

> ASK THE LORD, "IS THERE ANYTHING IN YOUR WORD I'M NOT LIVING OUT?" JOURNAL WHAT HE SHOWS YOU.

Word Search

Psalm 119:11, 41-48; Romans 12:2; Hebrews 4:12

Victory Strategy 28

One great way to seal truth in your heart so you can live out Kingdom Culture is to do a **"Word Search."**

Look up in a concordance all the passages that have to do with your issue. For example, if you struggle with pride, you might look up "pride," "proud," "haughty," "arrogant," but also the opposites, "humble," "humility," "meek," "serve," "servant."

For several of my strongholds, including pride, a Word Search was the gunpowder God used to blow up the walls. Why? How powerful is the Word? See Hebrews 4:12 and 2 Timothy 3:16.

> DO A WORD SEARCH NOW ON AN ISSUE GOD'S BEEN SHOWING YOU. (THERE ARE FREE CONCORDANCES ONLINE.) JOURNAL WHAT YOU FEEL GOD SPEAKING TO YOUR HEART THROUGH THE VERSES THAT TOUCH YOU.
>
> DON'T WORRY IF IT TAKES YOU AWHILE. MY JOURNEY TO FREEDOM FROM PRIDE TOOK MORE THAN A YEAR, AND MY WORD SEARCH ON "LOVE" TOOK 3-4 YEARS. JUST GO AT THE PACE GOD HAS FOR YOU IN YOUR QUIET TIMES, SO YOU CAN LEARN EVERYTHING HE'S TEACHING YOU. SPREAD IT OUT, JUST LOOKING UP A FEW VERSES A DAY, OR START WITH A QUICK SCAN OF ALL THE VERSES, ASKING GOD TO POINT YOU TO THE MOST IMPORTANT ONES.

James 2:14-17

- [ ] *talking about how important the Word is without spending time in it*
- [ ] *"faith" without deeds*
- [ ] *false compassion*
- [ ] *talking the talk without walking the walk*
- [ ] *doing what I want instead of looking for what God wants me to do*
- [ ] *talking about how important God is, but not spending time with Him*

29 Victory strategy

Daily quiet times

Luke 10:38-42; Hosea 2:14-16; Matthew 22:37

Ephesians 6:18

- ☐ distracted while praying
- ☐ worrying with my eyes closed, not praying in faith
- ☐ bored with prayer
- ☐ ceasing from prayer
- ☐ not praying for others
- ☐ compartmentalizing — attending church or having a quiet time, then going about my day doing what I want rather than seeking God
- ☐ not standing on alert; letting the enemy sneak up on me and take me captive to do his will
- ☐ stuck in a prayer rut or ritual
- ☐ feeling like God's not hearing me
- ☐ not giving my every moment to Jesus

When you're in love with someone, you want to spend time with him, to be near him, to do things together.

You have time for what you make time for.

And yet, **too often we miss God's sweet plans for us because we're too busy to stop and just *be* with Him.**

Don't be like the wife who runs around all stressed out trying to serve her husband perfectly, without ever stopping to find out what he even wants. What if you're slaving over a steak, trying to make it just right, when he doesn't care what you cook? What if he's been trying for weeks just to have a moment with you so he could tell you his *vacation* plans for both of you?

Your Heavenly Husband didn't choose you to be His bride because He wanted a slave. **He wants relationship. He loves you.** Jesus has so many sweet, beautiful, amazing adventures planned for you to enjoy together. *Even times of rest.*

But if you're too busy to enjoy Him, to listen to His heart, to feel His touch, ... you'll miss out on what all this is for.

And you'll lose a lot of battles. Because *He's* the King Who rescues you, Who empowers you, Who arms you, Who trains you for war, Who protects you, Who gives you just the instructions you need to overcome. Psalm 18.

You *need* Him. *Desperately.*

> PLAN TIME TO BE ALONE WITH THE LORD EVERY DAY — I RECOMMEND AT LEAST 30 MINUTES, BUT 1-2 HOURS IS BEST — AND MAKE THAT YOUR HIGHEST PRIORITY. STUDY THE WORD, WORSHIP, PRAY, LISTEN FOR GOD'S VOICE, OR DO WHATEVER ELSE HE'S LEADING YOU TO DO, BUT ...
>
> **DON'T GO A DAY WITHOUT INVITING GOD INTO IT.**

Personal spiritual retreats

Luke 21:37; Matthew 14:23; Luke 6:12

Victory Strategy 30

If you're married, you know how important honeymoons and date weekends are with your husband. Well, your Heavenly Husband also wants to spend quality extended times with you.

I recommend setting aside a day once a month or a half-day every 1-2 weeks. But more is always better.

I love to hike with the Lord, worship Him at sunrise on the beach, and other such adventures. But one of my favorite things to do is to overnight at a friend's house while she's away. That way I have the whole place to myself, and I can worship, dance, sing at the top of my lungs, spread my study helps all over the room, watch the sunrise with the One I love, or do whatever else He's wanting to do together with me.

These extended times with God have been markers in my life, times when He has answered a question, given me direction for the next season, or taught me something infinitely important from His Word that I needed not just for the next battle, but *for the rest of my life.*

But don't just take my word for it. Jesus also was in the habit of getting away to be alone with God for extended times. And they were *One!* How much more I also need to spend time with my Father to become like Him.

If you're not sure what to do for a personal retreat, feel free to write me at MoreThanAConquerorBooks@gmail.com for ideas. And if your staff, team, friends, Bible study group, or other couples, women, youth, etc., would like to get away for 1-5 days and draw closer to the Lord together, I'm happy to help tailor-make a One Retreat (for oneness with Christ and with each other). Visit the "Retreat" page at www.MoreThanAConquerorBooks.com, or write MoreThanAConquerorBooks@gmail.com for more information.

Psalm 10:4
- [ ] not seeking God
- [ ] pushing God out of my life
- [ ] avoiding quiet times
- [ ] distracted
- [ ] filling my thoughts with other matters, so there's no room for God
- [ ] avoiding God

Mal. 3:8-10
- [ ] robbing God by not giving tithe
- [ ] _____
- [ ] _____
- [ ] _____
- [ ] _____

> PLAN YOUR NEXT EXTENDED TIME WITH GOD, AND GET READY FOR AN EXPERIENCE THAT JUST MIGHT CHANGE YOUR LIFE!

31 | Victory Strategy

Listen UP before deciding

Proverbs 3:5-7; John 5:19, 10:27, 14:15; Jeremiah 29:11-13

Proverbs 3:5-7

- ☐ spending time on things that don't matter
- ☐ doing things my own way
- ☐ stressed out
- ☐ pressured
- ☐ letting busyness overtake God's purposes for me
- ☐ not following God's plan for me
- ☐ not seeking God because I don't believe He will answer
- ☐ relying on my own ability, knowledge, or experience, rather than trusting in God's
- ☐ leaning on my own understanding of a situation rather than seeking God's viewpoint
- ☐ unwise decision-making processes

How do you make decisions? Do you weigh the pros and cons? Press for what you want? Lean on your own understanding and experience? Ask others their opinions on the matter?

Our decision-making processes are one of the main ways the enemy slips in to do his dirty work. *We're in a hurry. We think we already know best. We lean on our own experience or skills. We're afraid. We have to take this step to succeed. We don't want to disappoint someone. We have no choice. We want this so badly we don't care what God wants....* Do any of those methods feel familiar to you?

Proverbs 3:5-6 urges us to stop leaning on our own understanding and seek the Lord's guidance in **ALL** our ways. It's not just the big decisions we are to pray about. It's *every* decision that needs to be handed to God.

Whether or not you think you hear God answer, practice giving Him your every thought, every moment, every decision. *Practice surrender.*

The more you seek Him, surrender, and obey, the louder you'll hear His voice and the more His Spirit will flow through you in increasing measures, until walking as one with Him is normal, and doing things your own way feels awkward, uncomfortable, *wrong*.

But if you don't bother to seek Him before making daily decisions, you may not be able to find Him when you need Him most. And your pride might take you into some serious enemy territory. Isaiah 55:6, Jeremiah 29:11-13.

So stay close to your Shepherd. Lean on Him for everything. And He will lead you to the sweet pastures of His presence, love, and empowering; not to mention make every moment a God-awesome one! John 10:1-27, Psalm 23, Jeremiah 50:7.

> PRACTICE SEEKING THE LORD BEFORE EVERY DECISION TODAY, EVEN THE SMALL ONES, LIKE WHAT TO EAT, WHAT TO BUY AT THE STORE, OR WHICH ROUTE TO TAKE HOME FROM WORK. DON'T WORRY IF YOU CAN'T HEAR HIM STRAIGHT AWAY. JUST PRACTICE SURRENDERING TO HIM.

Body structure
1 Corinthians 12; Romans 12:1-10

Victory Strategy 32

In the New Testament picture of the body of Christ, each of the members listens to the Head, using his/her unique gifts to obey Him together as one.

No members are more important because their gifts are more visible. In fact, the hidden parts are vital. An apostolic foot, a helping hand, and a preaching mouth all need the intercessor heart and prophetic lungs pumping and breathing the Spirit's life and breath into the body. *We need each other.*

But what would happen if a shoulder took over, someone high up who isn't listening to the Head or to the members below him who are listening to the Head? He might cut off the body parts he doesn't see as necessary, or force feet to do things Christ never intended them to. Discouragement sets in fast when wives, family members, or Christian workers feel unheard or forced to do something contrary to what God has called them to. Such top-down decision-making can bring a body down.

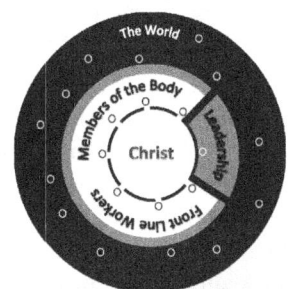

Leadership gifts do not replace the Head. Rather, leaders are to listen to Christ, follow His lead, and influence others to do the same.

Prov. 3:5-7 ...
- ☐ not asking questions to find out the facts first before deciding
- ☐ making unwise decisions
- ☐ making uninformed or misinformed decisions
- ☐ not seeking God's lead
- ☐ doing what others expect instead of what God wants
- ☐ saying yes to tasks God hasn't asked me to do
- ☐ _____
- ☐ _____

WALKING AS ONE WITH CHRIST AND WITH THE BODY BEGINS WITH YOU.

DO YOU TEACH A BIBLE STUDY? ARE YOU A MOTHER? WHAT OTHER WAYS DO YOU INFLUENCE OTHERS? ARE YOU LISTENING TO THE HEAD AND OBEYING HIM? HOW ARE YOU INFLUENCING OTHERS TO LISTEN AND OBEY? SPEND SOME TIME IN CONVERSATION WITH THE LORD ON THIS SUBJECT, AND JOURNAL WHAT HE SHOWS YOU.

Victory Strategy 33: Modeling body structure
John 5:19; Proverbs 3:5-6; 2 Timothy 2:2

Prov. 3:5-7 ...
- ☐ making decisions apart from God out of
- ☐ fear
- ☐ dread
- ☐ guilt
- ☐ pressure
- ☐ what I think others expect
- ☐ pride
- ☐ ambition
- ☐ experience
- ☐ inexperience
- ☐ ability
- ☐ inability
- ☐ habit
- ☐ tradition
- ☐ culture
- ☐ gossip, slander
- ☐ others' perceptions
- ☐ feelings
- ☐ stress
- ☐ laziness
- ☐ what feels good
- ☐ what seems right
- ☐ goals
- ☐ deadlines
- ☐ misinformation
- ☐ imaginations

One of the main reasons we have trouble walking out the Word in certain areas of our lives is **we've never seen it modeled.** Few of us have walked together through life with a mentor, like Jesus' disciples did with Him.

What does it look like to *pray without ceasing* (Ephesians 6:18 and 1 Thessalonians 5:17), to *only do what the Father is doing* (John 5:19), or to *seek God in all your ways?* (Proverbs 3:5-6) Whether you've seen someone else do it yet or not, **there are ways you can influence others to listen to God by modeling it yourself:**

- Before you read the Bible with your children or those you're teaching, **invite them to ask God to speak to them through His Word**. This changes horizontal expectations ("I wonder what she's going to tell us about God today") to vertical relationship ("Lord, what do YOU want to say to me today?")

- Let your children and others see you **pray first before making a decision.** Don't be afraid to say, "Let me pray about that and get back to you," or, "Hold on one moment while I ask the Lord."

- In fact, **invite those who will be affected by your decisions to listen to God together with you:**
  1) to **lay down their opinions or agendas at Jesus' feet.**
  2) to pray together with you, **asking God what He wants to do.**
  3) *then* (after surrendering and listening to God) **talk about the options** together, trusting God to lead. Don't be surprised if everyone hears Him say the same thing! But if opinions differ, look for how they fit together. He may want you to do *both* somehow.

- And don't just give advice. Ask the person to **seek God** together with you for what He wants to say first. **Then share** the verse, experience, or whatever other advice backs up what God is saying to them.

> IS GOD ASKING YOU TO DO ANY OF THESE THINGS IN A SITUATION YOU KNOW ABOUT?
>
> STEP OUT IN OBEDIENCE, AND WRITE YOUR EXPERIENCE IN YOUR JOURNAL.

Let God be Time Manager

Philippians 4:13; Proverbs 3:5-7; Ecclesiastes 3:1

Victory strategy 34

In all things Kingdom Culture, Jesus is our Model. And *Jesus only did what His Father was doing.* John 5:19.

So should we. **Burnout happens when you're doing more than God has asked you to, or** *you're doing it in your own power.*

That's why it's so important to surrender your schedule over to the Lord and let Him show you what *He* wants to do — not just sometimes, but *all* the time. Proverbs 3:5-7.

If you don't, you leave a wide-open door for the enemy to distract you with busy tasks that keep you from the powerful, meaningful, *eternal*, make-a-huge-difference things God wants to do.

So many times, if I'd gone ahead with what I had planned instead of asking Jesus what He wanted to do, I would have missed that woman at the market who was hungry to hear the Good News, or that hurting friend who showed up at my door unexpected, or a difficult circumstance my children needed help through....

The every-day moments I hand to God become God-awesome moments in His hand!

Prov. 3:5-7 ...
- [ ] making decisions apart from God out of
- [ ] busyness
- [ ] suspicion
- [ ] financial gain
- [ ] saving face
- [ ] personal gain
- [ ] jealousy
- [ ] sin habits
- [ ] wanting to get back at someone
- [ ] wanting to feel accepted
- [ ] _____
- [ ] _____
- [ ] _____
- [ ] _____
- [ ] _____
- [ ] _____

> TAKE THE TIME TO HAND THIS SEASON TO GOD. WHAT DOES HE WANT YOU TO BE BUSY WITH? ASK HIM. MATTHEW 22:37-40. IS THERE ANYTHING YOU'RE DOING HE HASN'T ASKED YOU TO?
>
> IS THERE ANYTHING HE'S ASKED YOU TO DO YOU HAVEN'T DONE YET? WHAT'S KEEPING YOU FROM OBEDIENCE? ASK HIM. WRITE IN YOUR JOURNAL WHAT HE SHOWS YOU.

If you'd like to build in new lifestyle habits for letting God be your Time Manager, the ***Delight to Be a Woman of Wonder Power Planner*** daily calendar agenda, goal planner is now available at www.MoreThanAConquerorBooks.com.

35 Victory Strategy

First thought: Jesus

Isaiah 50:4; Psalm 139:17-18; Psalm 57:8; Psalm 108:2

Prov. 3:5-7 …

- ☐ saying no because I feel incapable or too busy
- ☐ forgetting about God
- ☐ not handing my time or schedule to God
- ☐ leaning on my own understanding to discipline my children
- ☐ seeing some decisions as too small to ask God first before making them
- ☐ running through my busy day without inviting God into it
- ☐ doing things as I see fit throughout the day
- ☐ forgetting about God
- ☐ people pleasing
- ☐ making decisions before I seek God about it

Before you open your eyes, before you think of all the things you have to do, before you feel the pressure of the coming battles, before you get out of bed … think *Jesus*.

And **hand Him your day.**

Here are some ideas for those first thoughts:

- Lord, my day is yours, and so am I, to do with me as You will.
- What do You want to do today? I want to join You there.
- Do You have a word for me today?
- Is there something You want to show me or teach me?
- What verses will I need for what I will face today?
- Lord, how do You want me to bless my husband (roommate, children, mother, father, friend, rival, etc.)?
- Is there anything on my schedule that's not what You have planned? Or anything You want to add to it?
- Lord, would You please delight me with Your love today? Do something so intimate, so personal, so loving, so surprising, only You would know how to do that.

The more you seek God, the easier it will be to hear His voice and follow His lead. Don't worry if you can't discern His answer right away. Just keep your questions open before Him. And remember He speaks in many ways, not just the way you're expecting Him to (See Strategy 12).

> TOMORROW MORNING, AND EVERY DAY, **MAKE JESUS YOUR FIRST THOUGHT.**
>
> BY THE TIME YOU'RE UP AND HAVE HAD YOUR QUIET TIME, HE PROBABLY WILL HAVE GIVEN YOU A VERSE, A SONG, A THOUGHT (LIKE, "TRUST ME"), INSTRUCTIONS, SOMETHING HE'S PREPARING YOU FOR OR GROWING YOU IN, SOMETHING TO LOOK FOR FROM HIM (LIKE A SWEET DEMONSTRATION OF HIS LOVE), ETC.
>
> LET THAT GUIDE YOU THROUGHOUT THE DAY, AS YOU LOOK FOR HIM TO DO THAT, AND FOLLOW WHERE HE'S LEADING. THEN, AT NIGHT, WRITE IN YOUR JOURNAL YOUR EXPERIENCES WITH HIM.

The *Delight to Be a Woman of Wonder Day Planner*, at www.MoreThanAConquerorBooks.com, is designed to do this every day for a year.

Lord of the day

James 4:8; 2 Corinthians 10:3-5; Isaiah 55:6-12

Victory Strategy 36

After building into my daily lifestyle Strategy 35 (making Jesus my first thought) for several years, something amazing happened. *God Himself* started waking me up every morning. *As if He couldn't wait to tell me what He wanted to do that day.* **As if He couldn't wait to** *be with me.*

Sometimes, He awakens me with a song, a word, a verse, a dream, a vision, instructions for the day, or just some sweet demonstration of His love. But I've found, **when my day starts with Jesus, it's a powerful day!**

One morning, He woke me up with specific instructions to call so-and-so at 8:30, be in that village by 11, go together to another village.... I followed His schedule exactly, and *eight people came to Christ that day!*

How many miracles do we miss by forgetting to hand our day to Jesus?

Again, this lifestyle of walking in deep intimacy with Christ, where He talks to us, guides us, and does amazing things we could never do on our own, doesn't happen overnight. *We have to purpose to draw near to Him so He will draw near to us.*

That starts with handing Him your day, then looking for what He's doing all throughout the day, inviting Him into every moment, handing Him your thoughts, and asking Him His opinion on every circumstance.

At first it feels awkward to hand God every situation. But, just like making Jesus my first thought each morning, once it becomes a habit, the Spirit takes over. Then walking in His power becomes so normal, stepping *outside* of His leading is what feels awkward.

Prov. 3:5-7 ...
- [ ] only seeking God sometimes, not in "all" my ways.
- [ ] not taking time to talk and pray together with those who will be affected by my decisions before I make them
- [ ] running over people or God to reach a goal
- [ ] not modeling for my children and others I lead listening to God before making decisions

> TOMORROW MORNING, HAND YOUR DAY TO JESUS, THEN WALK OUT INTO IT TALKING TO HIM, LISTENING FOR HIS VOICE, ASKING HIM TO SHOW YOU WHAT HE'S DOING, AND JOINING HIM THERE. AT NIGHT, WRITE IN YOUR JOURNAL WHAT HE DID.

37 Victory Strategy

Lord of the night

Psalm 92:1-2; 1 Chronicles 23:30; Psalm 4:4; 63:6; 119:148

Prov. 3:5-7 ...

- ☐ self-pleasing
- ☐ making a decision without looking for truth or listening to those who know the situation best and listen to God
- ☐ giving advice without seeking God for His first
- ☐ _____
- ☐ _____
- ☐ _____
- ☐ _____

2 Timothy 1:7

- ☐ indecision
- ☐ self-judging
- ☐ intimidation
- ☐ shame
- ☐ embarrassment
- ☐ self-abasement
- ☐ cowardice
- ☐ claustrophobia
- ☐ agoraphobia (fear of open or crowded spaces)

How you sleep most often has to do with the condition of your mind and heart.

The more your thoughts line up with Truth, the more at peace you will be when you lie down to sleep at night.

That's why it's so important to seek the Lord for **freedom from anxiety, fear,** and other strongholds (Strategies 25, 51, 52).

Tips for handing your night to God:

1. Lean in for a **goodnight kiss**. (Strategy 26)
2. Pray for **protection over your dreams.** (Strategy 38)
3. Don't pray worry prayers that make you anxious or fretful. *The enemy is not all-powerful* and *he is definitely not sovereign.* So, trust in the One Who loves you and has everything under His control. Seek Him for what He's doing, and follow the **Philippians 4 Plan for Peace** (Strategy 40).
4. The "**watches of the night**" are a sweet time for intimacy with God. The house is still. No distractions, nothing that has to be done right then, ... just ... rest ... in the arms of the One you love ... and *enjoy Him.*
5. "Soak" in **soft worship** music, listening to the words, letting God sing over you and soothe your heart as you fall asleep.
6. If you wake up in a panic or under attack, you may need to do some warfare. **Tell the enemy to go, invite Jesus to fill the room with His presence**, and **worship.** (Strategy 52)
7. Seek **healing for nightmares.** (Strategy 39)
8. Pray for **Kingdom matters.** (Strategy 86)
9. You may be awake for a reason. **Ask the Lord and listen for His leading.** (1 Samuel 3:8-10)

> TONIGHT AS YOU GO TO SLEEP, TRY ONE OR MORE OF THE ABOVE TIPS TO HAND YOUR NIGHT TO GOD, THEN TOMORROW WRITE IN YOUR JOURNAL WHAT GOD DID WITH YOUR NIGHT.

Protection prayer

Psalm 4:8; 91; 127:2

Victory strategy 38

In the country where we live and work, most of our neighbors worship demons. Because of the intense spiritual warfare that brings about, praying protection over our family and our dreams is a *must*.

Every night, before we sleep, we pray together with our children something like this, *"Lord, please wrap Your arms around us all night long and give us sweet dreams from Your heart to ours. Guard us from evil dreams, and don't let us wake up until it's time to wake up in the morning. Put Your angels all around our home and fill every room with Your presence. Protect us and all our things from any harm...."*

When a business moved in next door, we noticed they parked their vehicles in our carport instead of theirs. When my husband asked them why, they said, "When we park them at ours, they get stolen. But when we park them at yours, they don't."

We may not be able to see with our eyes what's happening in the spiritual realm, but prayer most certainly makes a difference.

> GET IN THE HABIT OF PRAYING FOR PROTECTION OVER YOUR HOME, FAMILY AND DREAMS BEFORE YOU GO TO SLEEP EACH NIGHT.

2 Tim. 1:7 ...
- [ ] *fear of*
  - [ ] mirrors
  - [ ] reproof
  - [ ] disapproval
  - [ ] disappointment
  - [ ] the dark
  - [ ] death
  - [ ] the future
  - [ ] flying
  - [ ] heights
  - [ ] being noticed
  - [ ] not being noticed
  - [ ] people
  - [ ] speaking truth in love
  - [ ] drowning
  - [ ] ghosts
  - [ ] pain
  - [ ] pregnancy
  - [ ] crime, burglars, attackers

39 Victory Strategy

Cleanse that nightmare

Psalm 139:8; Song of Songs 3:6-8; Psalm 45:3-5; John 8:32

2 Tim. 1:7 ...

- ☐ fear of
  - ☐ fear
  - ☐ work
  - ☐ sleep
  - ☐ nightmares
  - ☐ devil or demons
  - ☐ dolls
  - ☐ clowns
  - ☐ food
  - ☐ choking
  - ☐ opinions (hearing what others think of me)
  - ☐ talking on the phone
  - ☐ depths (lakes, tunnels, caves)
  - ☐ light
  - ☐ fire
  - ☐ rain
  - ☐ storms
  - ☐ wind
  - ☐ thunder
  - ☐ lightning
  - ☐ the ocean
  - ☐ bridges
  - ☐ being buried alive
  - ☐ hospitals
  - ☐ rape
  - ☐ getting old
  - ☐ roller coasters
  - ☐ the unknown
  - ☐ public speaking

Because the God Who loves me is Sovereign and because I've asked Him to protect my dreams each night, *if I have a nightmare, then I assume He has allowed it for a reason.*

Sometimes He allows a nightmare to reveal to me some way Satan has been picking on our family or others. Then I can pray for them and fight for them.

Other times, God allows me to see some issue in my own heart that needs to be dealt with.

Here is a powerful way, similar to the Truth Encounter (Strategy 18), to invite God's healing and cleansing for your nightmares:

1. Go back into the memory of your nightmare together with the Lord, especially whatever scene most distressed you.

2. What did you feel when that happened? Follow those feelings to find the lies.

3. Now, ask God for His truth. He may speak a verse or something from His heart to your heart, or He may even *transform* your dream.

For example, once I dreamed my daughter was laughing and leaning on me. But, knowing I couldn't support her weight, I moved out of the way. She fell and died quite graphically.

I woke up feeling I'm not there for her; I don't support her enough; I'm a bad mom. I hadn't even realized I had been thinking those thoughts, but the dream exposed them. When I went through the steps above, at the point in the dream where I had moved out of the way, Jesus caught her in His arms. He said to me, "You were never supposed to be the one she leans on. *I* am the One Who catches her when she falls."

> CAN YOU THINK OF A NIGHTMARE THAT WAS DISTRESSING TO YOU? SPEND SOME TIME WITH THE LORD WALKING THROUGH THE ABOVE STEPS WITH HIM, AND WRITE YOUR EXPERIENCE IN YOUR JOURNAL.

Philippians 4 Plan for Peace

Victory Strategy 40

Philippians 4:4-8; Romans 8:28

Do you sometimes lie awake at night with a million thoughts running through your head?

Philippians 4:4-8 offers a great guideline for such times:

1. Rejoice. **God is near!**
2. Whatever is worrying you, **hand it to Him.**
3. Ask for His help and **thank Him** for the outcome (even though you don't know what it is yet). *He can bring the good out of every situation.* Romans 8:28. In fact, **thank Him for everything He's done for you.**
4. Rest in His **peace,** and **think on Jesus** — His truth, majesty, righteousness, holiness, beauty, power, excellence — *for He is worthy of praise.*
5. So **worship Him.**

Worship sends the enemy to flight. (Strategy 99) He can't stand to be in the same room when we worship God.

I actually used this method for the first time when I was 11 years old without even realizing it. In a Third World country at a camp for missionary kids, the adults put me in a room with much younger children and no counselor, probably hoping I'd be a good influence on them.

At night, we heard rats scurrying around and other disturbing noises. All the girls crowded into my bed, afraid. I didn't know what to do, so I prayed. Then we took turns thanking God. And we sang praise songs to Him.

As His peace settled over the room, each child went back to her bed and slept all night.

2 Tim. 1:7 ...
- ☐ *fear of*
- ☐ *spiders*
- ☐ *chickens*
- ☐ *bugs*
- ☐ *mice*
- ☐ *dogs*
- ☐ *birds*
- ☐ *roaches*
- ☐ *fish*
- ☐ *bats*
- ☐ *bees*
- ☐ *wasps*
- ☐ *snakes*
- ☐ *moths*
- ☐ *ants*
- ☐ *frogs*
- ☐ *worms*
- ☐ *sharks*
- ☐ *horses*
- ☐ *insects*
- ☐ *other animals:*
- ☐ _____
- ☐ _____
- ☐ _____
- ☐ _____
- ☐ _____
- ☐ _____

WHAT THOUGHTS HAVE WORRIED YOU LATELY? STEP THROUGH PHILIPPIANS 4 ABOVE, WRITING IN YOUR JOURNAL ALL THE THINGS YOU'RE THANKFUL FOR.

A THANKFUL HEART BRINGS PEACE.

41 Victory Strategy

Trust God's sovereignty

Romans 8:28; Matthew 7:7-11; Hosea 2:14-20; John 16:33

2 Tim. 1:7 ...

- ☐ fear of
  - ☐ being alone
  - ☐ men
  - ☐ women
  - ☐ love
  - ☐ intimacy
  - ☐ marriage
  - ☐ divorce
  - ☐ commitment
  - ☐ abandonment
  - ☐ change
  - ☐ being forgotten
  - ☐ not remembering
  - ☐ accusation
  - ☐ authority
  - ☐ getting rid of stuff
  - ☐ technology
  - ☐ driving
  - ☐ Halloween
  - ☐ number 13
  - ☐ Friday the 13th
  - ☐ evil omens
  - ☐ terrible things happening
  - ☐ vomiting
  - ☐ blood
  - ☐ holes
  - ☐ making wrong decisions
  - ☐ accidents
  - ☐ failure

God is Sovereign. *Let that be your anchor in times of trouble.* He knows what He's doing, and **He loves you.**

So, whatever trial you are going through, don't let your mind head off in wrong directions. You don't know what's up ahead. You can't see yet what God's doing in the midst of all this. No matter how terrible your troubles are, whether death or hunger or illness or abuse or demonic attacks or whatever else plagues you, *God is greater.* And *He will see you through.*

Nothing can happen to you that God hasn't allowed. And if He has allowed it, then it is for a reason.

When I lost a baby, I never imagined all the women God would use me to comfort through their own losses, or the sweet things God would do in my quiet times to draw me closer to Him and help me understand so much more about what it was like for Him to lose His Son.

And when I was struck with a terrible disease that should have left me blind and bed-ridden the rest of my life, I never imagined how He would transform my heart and then heal me. And how God would use the lessons I learned through that experience to mentor many other people and see their lives transformed, as well.

Death, sickness, accidents, and other traumatic experiences will happen to all of us who live long enough to see it, for such is this fallen world. But have faith, for **the One Who has overcome the world lives within you, overcomer.**

IN WHAT WAYS HAS YOUR MIND RUN OFF IN WRONG DIRECTIONS THROUGH THE TRIAL YOU'RE IN RIGHT NOW? HAVE YOU WORRIED? TRIED TO CONTROL THINGS? FELT ANGRY AT GOD? DESPAIRED?

JOURNAL YOUR THOUGHTS, AND HAND THEM OVER TO THE LORD, TRUSTING THAT HE LOVES YOU AND HAS A LOVING PLAN THROUGH IT ALL.

Turn to God, not away
James 4:7-8; Job 3, 42; 1 Corinthians 10:13

Victory strategy 42

Don't make the mistake of turning your back on God or avoiding Him during your trial because you're angry or you think He's not listening to you.

Remember that *whatever you're going through, the enemy's prime objective in attacking you is to draw you away from God.*

So **do the opposite of what the enemy wants you to:** ***Draw near.***

If you're angry because you feel God is unloving to make you or someone you love go through this, then *tell Him that.* Beat on His chest, like Job did, if you need to. But turn *to* Him, not away. His chest is broad enough, His love deep enough. If you need to have a meltdown, *in His arms* is the best place to do it.

God loves you, and whatever pain you're feeling, He's feeling it too. He was there when that person said that, when you were betrayed, when no one was there for you in your darkest trial, and He felt your heart, heard your thoughts. He loves you. He is *for* you.

> NO MATTER HOW HARD THINGS ARE, TURN TO THE LORD. LET HIM HOLD YOU, COMFORT YOU, HEAL YOU, TRANSFORM YOU, AND USE YOU TO DRAW OTHERS INTO HIS ARMS THROUGH THIS TRIAL.

2 Tim. 1:7 ...
- ☐ *fear of*
- ☐ poverty
- ☐ success
- ☐ germs, bacteria
- ☐ responsibility
- ☐ rejection
- ☐ not being loved or liked
- ☐ judgment
- ☐ being wrong
- ☐ fat people (usually affects anorexics, bulimics)
- ☐ feet
- ☐ crowds
- ☐ falling
- ☐ needles
- ☐ the end of the world
- ☐ not protecting loved ones

43 Victory Strategy

Look for God's plan
John 5:19; Romans 8:28

2 Tim. 1:7 ...
- ☐ fear of
  - ☐ hugs
  - ☐ those who are close to God
  - ☐ being on the wrong path
  - ☐ what God will tell me to do if I surrender
- ☐ other unholy fear of God: _____
- ☐ other fears:
  - ☐ _____
  - ☐ _____
  - ☐ _____

Proverbs 29:25
- ☐ fear of man

Isaiah 22
- ☐ fear of hardship
- ☐ running from trials
- ☐ self-protection
- ☐ self-defense
- ☐ breaking from God's plan to put my own in place
- ☐ feeling defeated
- ☐ giving up under attack

Whatever conflict you're in, whatever hardship you're going through, no matter how many evil, terrible things you see Satan doing, you can be sure **God *is doing more*.**

He's teaching you something new. He's shining His love through you to that other person. He's pushing you out of one season, opening a door to a new one. He's showing you a piece of His character you will need to trust in for a future battle. He's training you, strengthening your spiritual muscles, building in you a new gift, touching the hearts of those who are watching you go through this....

† But whatever God is doing, even if you can't see it clearly, know this: **God is always drawing you to Himself.** So, head that way, and you'll know you're headed in the right direction.

But sometimes the reason I can't see clearly what God's doing is because *I haven't asked Him*. But as soon as I ask Him, "Lord, what are You doing? I want to follow You there," He shows me.

Interesting, isn't it? Of course, it's not always so quick, but **we were created for divine relationship. And just like a marriage,** *if we do all the talking, we cannot truly know our Beloved's heart.*

> WHAT CONFLICT OR DIFFICULTY ARE YOU GOING THROUGH RIGHT NOW? ASK GOD WHAT HE'S DOING, AND FOLLOW HIM THERE.

Go opposite Satan's plan

James 4:7-8; Psalm 129:1-4; John 10:10; Psalm 119:133-134

Victory Strategy 44

It's often easier to see what Satan is doing in your trial than what God's doing. *He's dividing a friendship, sowing distrust in your husband, making you jealous, destroying what you've worked so hard for, keeping you too busy to pray, depressing you, frustrating you, angering you, making you give up....*

If you can't see what God is doing, at least

† **Purpose to do the opposite of what the enemy is doing.**

Rather than complain, *thank God*. Rather than withdraw, *reach out in love*. Rather than attack with your arguments, *listen*. Rather than thinking bitter thoughts, *forgive*. Rather than wallowing in self-pity or depression, *worship God*.

> WHAT IS THE ENEMY WANTING YOU TO DO IN THIS PRESENT TRIAL? WHAT WOULD IT LOOK LIKE TO DO THE OPPOSITE? ASK THE LORD, WRITE IN YOUR JOURNAL WHAT HE SHOWS YOU, AND PURPOSE TO WALK IN LOVE. MATTHEW 22:37-40.

Is. 22 ...
- ☐ wishing I was dead
- ☐ false prophesying
- ☐ declaring a negative outcome based on my fears
- ☐ not seeking, listening to, or obeying God's instructions
- ☐ throwing caution to the wind
- ☐ not interceding for others as they endure trials
- ☐ dropping responsibility
- ☐ unreliable
- ☐ poor leadership

45 Victory Strategy

Come up here

Romans 12:2; Psalm 40:2; Exodus 19:4; Isaiah 40:27-31

Philippians 4:1-13

- ☐ not standing firm
- ☐ disagreements
- ☐ discord
- ☐ disloyal
- ☐ depression
- ☐ overwhelming grief
- ☐ negative attitude
- ☐ pessimism
- ☐ joylessness
- ☐ letting a feeling of being far from God keep me from drawing near
- ☐ others can't see gentleness in me
- ☐ anxiety
- ☐ anxious heart
- ☐ tension
- ☐ stress
- ☐ nervousness
- ☐ fretfulness
- ☐ inability to relax
- ☐ inability to enjoy
- ☐ dread
- ☐ apprehension
- ☐ terror
- ☐ easily panicked
- ☐ hysteria

For six years straight, someone in our family died every six months. Even my pastor committed suicide. As if all those tragedies didn't cause enough grief, my best friends moved away and cut me out of their lives.

But Jesus ... He awakened me early each morning to hold me and heal me. One way He did that was through what I call "Come-up-here" moments.

When my feet are stuck in the muck of other people's junk (and my own, too!), and my problems are all up in my face, ... it's difficult to see anything else.

But then He whispers, "Come up here."

He lifts me out of the miry clay like only He can — not to rescue me so much as to *realign my heart with His*. **The problem is still there.** *It's my perspective He wants to change.*

In those "Come up here" moments, He might remind me of the trials His saints have endured through the centuries, showing me how my tiny difficulty is but a slender thread in a vast, intricate tapestry He's weaving as He draws all nations to Himself.

Other times, He might show me something He's doing in my heart or in others around me.

And sometimes He just sits with me, letting me feel His love, reminding me He's still Sovereign. He's still in control. He's still good. And His ways are still breathtakingly beautiful. *Even if nothing in my trial changes.*

But then there are those times when **He changes everything. He was just waiting for me to share His perspective first!**

> SHARE WITH GOD THE TRIALS YOU ARE GOING THROUGH RIGHT NOW, LAYING YOUR THOUGHTS AND FEELINGS AT HIS FEET. THEN ANSWER HIS INVITATION TO "COME UP HERE." ISAIAH 55. ASK HIM TO SHOW YOU WHATEVER HE WANTS TO SHOW YOU. THEN *FOLLOW HIM THERE.*

Wreck it in Jesus' arms

Philippians 4:8; 2 Corinthians 10:3-5

Victory strategy 46

Does your train of thoughts ever get off track?

There you are in your quiet time praying sweetly, but then suddenly, some person or event comes to mind, and too late, you realize your "train" has derailed and you're headed down the mountain to land at the bottom in a messy heap.

That's what I call a "train wreck," and it can happen at any time, not just in your quiet times.

But if you're going to have a train wreck, in God's presence is the best place to have it. **Hand those distressing thoughts to Him. Ask Him what He thinks about that situation or that person**. Let Him put your thoughts back on track, even if it takes a little while, even if you need to cry or vent or whatever.

But don't stay down there in the abyss. Ask the Lord how you got there, let Him show you the lies that led you to such emotions and thoughts, and let Him heal you, restore you, raise you back up, so you can walk out in the power of His High-way of love. Isaiah 35:8-10.

Phil. 4 …
- ☐ worry
- ☐ nervous habits, like overeating, jiggling leg or foot, biting nails …
- ☐ upheaval
- ☐ restlessness
- ☐ hyperactivity
- ☐ easily excited
- ☐ roving
- ☐ insomnia (due to overactive mind, worry, etc.)
- ☐ panic attacks
- ☐ not thanking God
- ☐ unthankful
- ☐ taking things into my own hands rather than seeking God

> DON'T LET THE ENEMY WIN. NOTICE WHEN YOUR TRAIN OF THOUGHTS STARTS TO DERAIL, AND HAND THOSE THOUGHTS TO THE LORD. ASK HIM HOW HE SEES THAT SITUATION OR THAT PERSON. PRAY FOR THEM. WORSHIP. SEEK GOD FOR A TRUTH ENCOUNTER. LET HIM PUT YOU BACK ON TRACK TO SWEET PLACES OF HIS LOVE, JOY, PEACE, AND FAITH.

47 Victory strategy

Don't get distracted
Psalm 42:1-2; 46:10

Phil. 4 ...

- ☐ prayerless
- ☐ ungrateful
- ☐ disgusted (but not over my own sin)
- ☐ not trusting God with my problems (worrying with my eyes closed rather than praying in faith)
- ☐ defeatism
- ☐ heaviness
- ☐ not letting Christ's peace guard my mind
- ☐ gloom
- ☐ sense of failure
- ☐ thinking on lies
- ☐ wrong thought processes
- ☐ wrong choices
- ☐ impure thoughts
- ☐ impure motives
- ☐ impure acts
- ☐ talking about others behind their backs
- ☐ unloving thoughts

If you're like most people, your days are so over-the-top busy that whenever you finally sit still for your quiet times, all kinds of thoughts that have been waiting to get your attention pounce upon your mind.

That phone call you need to make. That thing you forgot to do. What you need at the store. That meeting you don't want to forget....

Satan would love to distract you from your quiet times by **convincing you that something else is more important or timely.**

So, keep a notepad next to your Bible, and just write it down so you won't forget it later. Then go back to being still before the Lord.

Ask God to take you anywhere He wants to take you in your quiet times, and then follow His lead. If you're busy praying about something, and an incident or person comes to mind seemingly off-subject, don't feel frustrated that it's yet another distraction. If you asked the Lord to lead you, maybe that person is your next prayer subject.

And what about the phone calls, the, "Honey, where's my ...?" from your husband, and the "Mommy! I want...." from your kids? Because they're bound to come, just as soon as you sit down to be with the Lord.

Remember, the enemy's prime objective is to keep you from drawing near to the Lord. So, expect it and prepare for it. Turn off your phone and leave it in another room. Talk with your husband and children and tell them this is your special time with God. Ask them to help you guard it. And ask the Lord to guard it too. Even as you're walking toward your favorite prayer nook, ask the Lord to surround that place with His shield, to protect that time with Him, to cancel all distractions, and give you a sweet, long, deep drink of His Living Water.

> ASK THE LORD WHAT DISTRACTS YOU IN YOUR QUIET TIMES, AND UNDERLINE ANYTHING ON THIS PAGE THAT MIGHT HELP. IS THERE ANYTHING ELSE GOD'S ASKING YOU TO DO? TRY THAT TODAY IN YOUR QUIET TIME.

Let God Distract You
2 Corinthians 4:6-18

Victory Strategy 48

Too often, we let the things of this world distract us from the Lord. But what if we **let *God* distract us from the things of this world** instead?

When our daughter was about to graduate and we were preparing to move, in the midst of all the packing, graduation activities, good-byes, and a hundred other things on our plate, one of my supervisors handed me a massive writing project for a prayer calendar on unreached peoples she was putting together. I wanted to say outright, "There's no way! I don't have time." But instead, I answered, "I'll pray about that."

And I did. In my quiet time, I wrote out the first sentence, just to get a feel for where He was leading me. Three hours later, what should have taken several weeks of intensive labor *He had finished in one quiet time!*

I sat there stunned before Him. If I had said "no" because I was so busy with other activities, if I hadn't prayed, if I hadn't let Him distract me from all the earthly things I had to do, I would have missed the miracle, and the many thousands who read what His Spirit wrote that day and prayed for all those unreached people would have missed it too. And what about the lost who were prayed for by those thousands of prayer warriors?

> "Mary ... sat at the Lord's feet listening to what he said. But Martha was distracted by all the preparations that had to be made. She came to Him and asked, 'Lord, don't you care that my sister has left me to do the work by myself? Tell her to help me!' 'Martha, Martha,' the Lord answered, 'you are worried and upset about many things, but few things are needed — or indeed only one. Mary has chosen what is better, and it will not be taken away from her.'"
> Luke 10:39-42.

Phil. 4 ...
- [ ] negativity
- [ ] always in everybody's business
- [ ] bossy, telling others what to do
- [ ] coarse talk
- [ ] dirty jokes
- [ ] profanity, cursing
- [ ] seeking to get the latest gossip on someone's situation
- [ ] ugly thoughts
- [ ] spiritual barrenness
- [ ] thoughts that tear down or pick at minor flaws in others
- [ ] _____
- [ ] _____

> HOW DO THE THINGS OF THIS WORLD DISTRACT YOU FROM THE LORD? ASK THE LORD TO DISTRACT YOU INSTEAD WITH HIMSELF, AND POSITION YOURSELF TO SPEND YOUR THOUGHTS AND TIME ON THE THINGS THAT MATTER MOST. 2 CORINTHIANS 4:6-18.

49 Victory Strategy

Hunger for God

Psalm 42:1-2, 7, Ephesians 3:16-20; Jeremiah 29:11-13

Phil. 4 ...
- ☐ thinking on, having an obsession with, or being absorbed in movies about
- ☐ death
- ☐ horror
- ☐ violence
- ☐ gruesome acts
- ☐ morbid behavior
- ☐ zombies
- ☐ vampires
- ☐ black magic
- ☐ demons
- ☐ witchcraft
- ☐ sex
- ☐ infidelity
- ☐ soap opera
- ☐ perversion
- ☐ abuse
- ☐ assault
- ☐ prejudice
- ☐ hatred
- ☐ revenge
- ☐ mocking God
- ☐ _____
- ☐ _____
- ☐ _____
- ☐ weary in well-doing
- ☐ loneliness

Are you still having trouble breaking away from the busyness of life to be with the One you love every day?

Then here's a question for you: How hungry are you for more of the Lord?

"Is it always this hard getting to the King? ... Why do some make it quicker than others?"

"Have you ever seen a hungry briar mouse? ... Normally, briar mice are careful. They hide beneath leaves and logs, taking only what food they can get to unnoticed. But a starving briar mouse ... will cross a wide-open rock in full view of wind eagles, just to get to the morsel he wants. He will brave every danger, overcome every obstacle, because he knows *without that morsel he will die.*"

— from *Rescue from Darkness*, Book One
Chronicles of the Kingdom of Light

Are you that desperate for the Lord? Do you truly desire Him more than anything else? *Let your hunger propel you to seek and find what you're looking for in Him.*

No one gets everything she wants in this life, unless her desire is for the Lord. Then He will certainly satisfy her with Himself.

If you're having trouble feeling hunger for God, do you at least **hunger to hunger** for Him?

> EACH TIME YOU'RE TEMPTED TO EAT EXTRA BROWNIES, OR SETTLE FOR THAT MOVIE YOU REALLY SHOULDN'T WATCH, EACH TIME THIS WORLD TRIES TO PULL YOU AWAY FROM THE MORE, THE BETTER, THE ETERNAL THINGS THAT TRULY MATTER, TRY SAYING, "NO! JESUS, YOU'RE THE ONE I HUNGER FOR. COME AND SATISFY ME WITH YOUR LOVE." THEN STEP AWAY FROM THAT TEMPTATION AND PURPOSE TO WORSHIP, PRAY, READ THE BIBLE, OR GO FOR A WALK OUTSIDE WITH THE LORD INSTEAD.
>
> TELL GOD YOU HUNGER TO HUNGER FOR HIM, AND THEN WRITE IN YOUR JOURNAL HOW YOU SEE THAT HUNGER GROWING, AND HOW HE SATISFIES YOU WITH HIMSELF.

Fear of the Lord
Job 28:28; Isaiah 33:6

Victory Strategy 50

Some Christians don't want to get too close to God, for fear He'll do something embarrassing or uncomfortable. Others are afraid of what He will ask them to do.

Have you ever said, "Lord, I'll go anywhere You want me to go. Just don't send me to _____"?

We all have different ways we've been afraid of God, but if your fear drives you *away* from Him instead of *toward* Him, then you can be sure that "fear" has the enemy's fingerprints all over it!

True, biblical fear of the Lord is a **wonder and awe** of His holiness and majesty that humbles you such that you want to drop all your sin, fall at His feet in surrender, and worship Him alone. And it is a *lifestyle*. **The woman who fears the Lord walks so closely to Him she wouldn't dare step off His paths for fear of missing the blessings, the miracles, and the joy of His felt presence.**

> WHAT UNHOLY WAYS HAVE YOU BEEN AFRAID OF GOD? HOW HAS THAT DRAWN YOU FARTHER FROM HIM?
>
> ARE THERE WAYS YOU'RE NOT WALKING IN FEAR OF THE LORD? ASK HIM, AND WRITE IN YOUR JOURNAL WHAT HE SHOWS YOU. THEN SPEND SOME TIME IN REPENTANCE AND WORSHIP, SEEKING TO DRAW NEAR AND SURRENDER TO THE ONE YOU LOVE.

Phil. 4 ...
- ☐ laughing at others' coarse talk or dirty jokes
- ☐ taking what little information I know and building up a story about it, then repeating those imaginations to others or treating that person as if my story is true
- ☐ inability to cope
- ☐ timidity
- ☐ shyness
- ☐ feeling inadequate
- ☐ insecurity
- ☐ inferiority

51 Victory Strategy

Don't listen to fear
Psalm 112:7-8; Genesis 15:1; 1 John 4:18

Phil. 4 ...
- [ ] ineptness
- [ ] rejection
- [ ] feelings that others are rejecting me
- [ ] introspection
- [ ] brooding
- [ ] self-conviction
- [ ] self-rejection
- [ ] self-hate
- [ ] lack of motivation
- [ ] boredom
- [ ] compulsions
- [ ] irresponsibility
- [ ] untrustworthy
- [ ] fear of boredom
- [ ] obsessed with ideas, projects
- [ ] self-deceived
- [ ] self-criticism
- [ ] afraid to witness for Christ
- [ ] procrastination
- [ ] preoccupation with food
- [ ] comparing myself with others
- [ ] self-reward
- [ ] _____

Most of us struggle with some kind of fear, even if it's just fear of what others will think of us.

A great way to set dynamite around those prison walls is to do a **Word Search**. Look up "fear," "afraid," "anxious," "tremble," "terror," "troubled," etc. Then look up opposites, like: "faith," "trust," "peace," "refuge," "courage," "courageous," "mighty," "guard," "protect," "watch," "safe," etc. And because of 1 John 4:18, look up "love," as well. You may want a separate journal just for this Word Search because it's so expansive. But it's worth it to be free from fear.

> Ask God what your fears are (I've listed some common ones in the checklist on pages 46-52), and write them out on the left side of your journal, leaving room on the right for truth (page 106 in your *Delight to Be a Woman of Wonder Prayer Journal*.)
>
> As God shows you His truth through your Word Search, situations He walks you through, His voice, etc., fill in the right column. (See below.)
>
> Begin your Word Search today with a quick scan of all the verses with the words "fear," "afraid," and "tremble." Write in your journal the pattern you see.

Fear:	Truth
Fear of being rejected	*1 John 3:1. I am beloved, accepted, CHOSEN. Even Jesus was rejected, but He loved in return; so can I through His love.*

More keys to freedom from fear are found in *Delight to Be a Woman of God* and the children's book, *Out You Go, Fear!*, at www.MoreThanAConquerorBooks.com.

Out you go, Fear!

Ephesians 6:10-18; Matthew 8:16, 32; Psalm 149:5

Victory Strategy 52

Have you ever awakened in the night gripped with panic or fear? Have you ever felt something was in the room? Or have you actually seen demons?

We are in a real battle, and whether or not you see your enemy, *he is real.*

Children are especially sensitive to demonic activity, and yours might wake you up to tell you they see "monsters." Don't just answer, "There's no such thing," and send them off to their room to face those monsters alone. **Equip your children to overcome the enemy.**

I've actually written a book called, *Out You Go, Fear!* to walk children through a simple strategy they can use to send the enemy running and sleep in peace. We had to teach our own children this method, and by the time they were five or so, they could do it on their own and go back to sleep without waking us up.

But this strategy will help in your own life, as well:

1. Before you go to sleep, **ask God to fill your room with His angels and His presence,** to **send out anything that's not of Him**, to **fill your dreams with Himself**, and to **guard you from bad dreams and evil attacks**.
2. If you feel afraid or wake up in a panic, **tell fear to "Go! In the name of Jesus!"** Matthew 8:16, 32.
3. **Worship the Lord.** Worship invites God near and sends the enemy to flight. (If you often struggle with fear, you might want to listen to worship music throughout the day, and find some soft acoustic worship to sleep to every night.)

Phil. 4 ...
- ☐ compromise
- ☐ self-delusion
- ☐ false humility
- ☐ easily distracted
- ☐ missing the beauty in life
- ☐ feeling dejected
- ☐ downcast
- ☐ despondent
- ☐ neglecting assembling together with God's people
- ☐ disinterest in spiritual things
- ☐ daydreaming
- ☐ fantasies
- ☐ vain imaginations
- ☐ pretension
- ☐ listlessness

> TRY THIS METHOD TONIGHT AS YOU GO TO SLEEP, AND TOMORROW WRITE IN YOUR JOURNAL WHAT GOD DID.

53 Victory Strategy

Stronghold domino effect

Matthew 12:43-45; Ephesians 4:26-27

Phil. 4 ...

- ☐ escape through sleep, drugs, or alcohol
- ☐ passivity
- ☐ stoicism
- ☐ lethargy
- ☐ double-mindedness
- ☐ leaving God out of my thinking
- ☐ comparing myself to self-imposed standards
- ☐ striving
- ☐ self-condemnation
- ☐ wanting to punish others
- ☐ wanting to punish myself
- ☐ seeking others' approval
- ☐ fear of condemnation
- ☐ feeling God's commandments are burdensome
- ☐ feelings of unworthiness
- ☐ feeling like God doesn't want me
- ☐ feeling God can't use me

If you have a stronghold of fear, you might also struggle with anxiety, panic attacks, low self-esteem, people-pleasing, perfectionism, lack of trust, fear of failure, fear of man, and any other number of fears.

That's because once the enemy gets a foothold in one place, he branches out from there to build a whole maze of linked strongholds.

For example, those who walk in religious pride are also likely to be controlled by legalism, judgment, self-righteousness, condemnation, accusation, control, dissension, slander, lust, anger, factions, etc.

But no matter what your cluster of linked strongholds looks like, you can be sure **pride is at the heart of it.**

If you break free from anger, low self-esteem, or lust, you will experience a joyous measure of freedom, but not until your pride falls will you see the other strongholds come tumbling down like dominoes.

I've drawn a diagram below and penciled in a few of my old strongholds (I had more than 30), so you can see how they link. Pride built fear, then pride and fear built fear of rejection, etc.

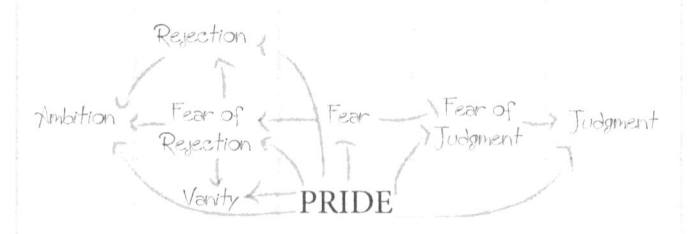

[Diagram: Rejection ↑ Fear of Rejection ← Fear → Fear of Judgment → Judgment; Ambition ← ; Vanity ← PRIDE]

> HAS GOD SHOWN YOU SOME OF YOUR STRONGHOLDS? IN YOUR JOURNAL, DRAW A SQUARE WITH BOXES, OR USE THE ONE ON PAGE 108 IN YOUR *DELIGHT TO BE A WOMAN OF WONDER PRAYER JOURNAL*. IN THE CENTER, WRITE "PRIDE." THEN WRITE YOUR OTHER STRONGHOLDS IN THE BOXES AROUND IT. HOW DOES PRIDE INFLUENCE THOSE? AND HOW DO THEY INFLUENCE EACH OTHER? ASK THE LORD, AND THEN DRAW ARROWS LINKING THEM, AND WRITE NOTES ABOUT THAT. CROSS OUT ANY STRONGHOLDS GOD HAS FREED YOU FROM.

Let grace free you

Romans 2:4; Luke 15:11-32; 2 Corinthians 7:11

Victory Strategy 54

If you feel condemnation as you discover sin and wrong thought processes, *it is not from God*. Romans 8:1.

There is a kind of Godly sorrow a repentant sinner experiences, but it is not like earthly sorrow or regret. **God's grace covers over our offenses with love, setting us free by making us "perfect," without blemish**, because of what Christ has done for us. Hebrews 10:14.

In fact, *God even brings good out of the messes we make.* Romans 8:28. That's how I can now write this book. If I'd never been a slave to sin, I'd never know how sweet freedom is or how to help others get there.

God convicts us of our sin, but He does so in **kindness** and **love**. His arms are open wide in **forgiveness** and **redemption**. His purpose is to **heal us, transform us,** and **restore us** to Himself.

He knows we can't do this on our own. ***We need His strength to overcome***. Philippians 4:13, Romans 8:28. Like a child just learning how to walk, we have a Father Who is here to pick us up, kiss our wounds, and help us get back up on our feet and try again. So we ***fix our eyes on Him and walk until we can run***. Hebrews 12:1-3.

Receive God's grace, and let Him set you free from regret and condemnation. Everyone makes mistakes. But through the power of grace, **a mistake is not a failure; it is *an opportunity to grow*** and see God do something beautiful.

Phil. 4 ...
- ☐ thinking I can't be forgiven by God
- ☐ feeling I would be the last one God would choose for anything
- ☐ feeling I must earn God's approval
- ☐ blaming God for what the devil or my own choices have caused
- ☐ questioning God
- ☐ mistrusting God
- ☐ dishonoring God
- ☐ feeling guilty
- ☐ idleness

> HOW ARE YOU DOING WITH RECEIVING GRACE? IF YOU STRUGGLE WITH FEELINGS OF CONDEMNATION, ASK GOD TO MEET YOU IN A TRUTH ENCOUNTER (STRATEGY 18), AND WRITE YOUR EXPERIENCE IN YOUR JOURNAL.
>
> IS THERE AN AREA OF YOUR LIFE WHERE YOUR SPIRITUAL "LEGS" ARE STILL A BIT WOBBLY? FIX YOUR EYES ON JESUS, GET UP AGAIN AND WALK.

Victory Strategy 55: Recognize pride's chains

Romans 12:3; Jeremiah 13:17; 1 John 2:16

Phil. 4 ...

- ☐ inability to trust
- ☐ not satisfied with the way God made me or my body
- ☐ not believing God loves me
- ☐ basing my salvation on my own worthiness
- ☐ confusion
- ☐ empty or worldly chatter
- ☐ not practicing what God has taught me
- ☐ seeing someone model Christ, but not following their lead
- ☐ not modeling Christ for others
- ☐ inability to be specific
- ☐ wishy-washy
- ☐ motivated by circumstances and feelings
- ☐ caring too much about what others think
- ☐ lover of the world

Pride closes the door on God's voice and opens the way for Satan to bend us to his will. But *humility draws us near to God and makes the enemy tremble.*

The world has a tendency to call us "humble" when we look down on ourselves or our abilities; and "proud" if we admit we're good at something.

In fact, one Christian told me, "I think moderation is the key. Don't think too high or too low of yourself; just somewhere in between."

But in Kingdom Culture, no matter how hard you try to even out your viewpoint, *you're still looking in the wrong direction if your eyes are on yourself.*

If you want to look at yourself, then look to God first. **Ask Him what He sees when He looks at you.** Only then will you have a clear view. If He calls you beautiful (Song of Songs 4:7), then you just are. To say anything else is to call Him a liar. **Agree with God. Surrender to Truth.** *Only when we align our thoughts with God's are we humbly seeing clearly.*

ASK GOD TO SPEAK TO YOUR HEART AS YOU LOOK UP IN A CONCORDANCE VERSES WITH THE WORDS, "PRIDE," "PROUD," "HAUGHTY," OR "ARROGANT." LIST IN YOUR JOURNAL SOME NEGATIVE EFFECTS OF PRIDE (DANGEROUS RESULTS, WAYS PRIDE AFFECTS YOUR LIFE, OTHERS' LIVES, AND YOUR RELATIONSHIP WITH GOD).

THEN WRITE SOME WORKING DEFINITIONS AND CHARACTERISTICS OF PRIDE GOD SHOWS YOU.

Let humility release you

2 Chronicles 7:14; James 4:10

Victory Strategy 56

If you do a Word Search (Strategy 28) on pride, you may experience a bit of fear of the Lord at seeing how many times God says He hates pride and will bring it down.

It's easier to walk in God's ways when you have a clear picture of where you're headed.

So, below, I've written some definitions of humility that God gave me to set me free from pride. These have now become "**life messages**" for me — *a message from God's heart to mine that's so important, I seek to live by it every day.*

Phil. 4 ...
- ☐ lover of pleasure
- ☐ no concern for those in need
- ☐ dissatisfaction
- ☐ disappointment
- ☐ discontentment
- ☐ unhappy
- ☐ hard to please
- ☐ particular
- ☐ spoiled
- ☐ demanding
- ☐ needy
- ☐ wasteful
- ☐ worldly
- ☐ materialistic
- ☐ shopaholic
- ☐ obsessed with money, food, or desire for possessions

Humility is...
- **Agreeing with God** (rather than believing what others say or what I think myself).
- **Remembering I am always in the presence of Someone greater.**
- **Dying to myself**, and **coming alive in Christ**. Galatians 2:20.
- **A servant's heart**. Philippians 2:1-8.
- **Complete surrender** to God, **depending on Him** for every thought, answer, and action. (This definition was the key to my freedom!).

> REMEMBER, KINGDOM DEFINITIONS DON'T ALWAYS MATCH THE WORLD'S, SO IT'S IMPORTANT TO LET THE WORD BE OUR GUIDE. WITH THAT IN MIND, LET'S CONTINUE OUR JOURNEY WITH A WORD SEARCH FOR "HUMILITY," "HUMBLE," AND "MEEK." WRITE IN YOUR JOURNAL THE DEFINITIONS GOD SHOWS YOU THAT TOUCH YOUR HEART, AS WELL AS POSITIVE RESULTS OF HUMILITY, SUCH AS THE ONE I'VE WRITTEN BELOW.

- Humility **draws me close** to God. Psalm 51:17.

If you'd like further studies on freedom from pride and other strongholds, try *Dare to Become a Kingdom Culture Leader, Volumes 1-2,* at www.MoreThanAConquerorBooks.com.

57 Victory strategy

Lay down pride and listen

Proverbs 13:10; James 1:19-20; 1 John 4:7-21

Phil. 4 ...
- [ ] sophistication
- [ ] stronghold of comfort
- [ ] couch potato
- [ ] social mediaholic
- [ ] TV-holic
- [ ] wasting time
- [ ] workaholic
- [ ] obesity
- [ ] compulsive eating
- [ ] addiction to sugar
- [ ] addiction to alcohol
- [ ] addiction to nicotine
- [ ] addiction to drugs
- [ ] addiction to sex
- [ ] other addictions: _____ _____ _____ _____
- [ ] self-inflicted harm, like cutting myself to get attention or to feel or not feel pain
- [ ] suppressing my true feelings

In the midst of a relationship conflict, most often we think the heart of the matter is, "He's not listening!" or "She's so mean to me!"

If he would just listen or *if she would just stop it,* the problem would be solved, right?

But regardless of the other person's junk, *your focus is what's creating the problem in you.*

You can't change that person, anyway, no matter how great your arguments are; only God can do that. But you *can* change your *own* heart, if you focus on the things that matter.

Lay down your rights. Lay down your selfishness. Lay down your need to be right. To be in control. To give a convincing argument. To be heard and understood. To be important.

Stop looking at what you want that other person to do, and listen. Try to understand. To have compassion. To love. To truly hear what she's saying and love her just as she is.

And **listen to God.** Ask Him what He's doing in the midst of this conflict. What does He want you to do? How does He want to use you to show His love?

Pride is at the heart of every conflict. If you obey it, you've lost the battle. But **love puts you on the winning side.** Matthew 22:37-40.

> WHAT CONFLICTS HAVE YOU BEEN IN LATELY? HAND THOSE OVER TO THE LORD, AND ASK HIM WHAT PART YOU PLAYED IN THE SITUATION. HOW WAS PRIDE INVOLVED, ESPECIALLY YOUR OWN? HOW CAN YOU DEMONSTRATE LOVE TO THAT PERSON? DO YOU NEED TO ASK FORGIVENESS? ASK GOD TO OPEN UP AN OPPORTUNITY TO DO THAT.
>
> **PRIDE IS AT THE HEART OF EVERY ARGUMENT. MAKE SURE IT'S NOT YOURS!**

Fight for others' freedom

Ephesians 6:10-18; 2 Corinthians 10:3-5; 1 Peter 4:8

Victory Strategy 58

What upsets you these days? What are you fighting about? If your purpose is to win an argument or get what you want, *you're fighting the wrong war.*

Remember, the battle is not for you to be understood or treated right. It's not to get others to agree with you or do what you want.

In fact, *your battle is not against people at all.*

You have a real enemy, but it's not your brother. So, fight *for* your brother, not against him.

Listen to what matters to your sister. Let her know she's not alone. Don't just judge her for her strongholds. Pray for her. **Fight for her freedom.**

Remember who your real enemy is and **choose to do the opposite of what he's urging you to do.** Rather than stewing in pain or anger, *pray* (even while that person's yelling at you). Rather than talking over others, *listen.* Rather than attacking, *seek to understand.* Look for what part you had in the situation, and be quick to *ask forgiveness.*

And above all, *love.* For love covers over a multitude of sins.

Phil. 4 ...
- ☐ inability to express true spiritual gifts
- ☐ self-destruction
- ☐ _____
- ☐ _____

Psalm 37
- ☐ fretting
- ☐ seething
- ☐ feeling others treat me unfairly
- ☐ nervous
- ☐ envious of sinners
- ☐ upset
- ☐ blowing things out of proportion
- ☐ not surrendering to God

> SIT WITH THE LORD FOR A MOMENT AND ASSESS YOUR THOUGHT LIFE TOGETHER WITH HIM. IN WHAT WAYS HAVE YOU BEEN JUDGMENTAL OR BITTER TOWARD OTHERS? TAKE THOSE THOUGHTS CAPTIVE AND TURN THEM INTO PRAYERS FOR THOSE PEOPLE'S FREEDOM.

For guides on helping your wife, children and others to freedom from strongholds, study *Dare to Be a Kingdom Culture Leader, Volumes 1-2,* available at **www.MoreThanAConquerorBooks.com**.

59 Victory Strategy

End to conflict starts in me
Proverbs 3:5-6, Isaiah 55:6-9; James 1:19, 4:11-12

Ps. 37 ...
- ☐ perturbed
- ☐ skipping quiet times
- ☐ lacking patience
- ☐ getting ahead of God to make something happen
- ☐ focusing on what I want or didn't get
- ☐ focusing on how others treat me
- ☐ proud
- ☐ pushy
- ☐ persecuting those who are righteous
- ☐ attacking God's people with words, thoughts, or actions
- ☐ greed
- ☐ not paying debts
- ☐ not giving to those in need

Romans 12:3
- ☐ thinking of myself higher than I ought
- ☐ looking down on others

How can you respond in the midst of conflict such that pride doesn't win? Here are a few keys:

† When you feel your emotions rising, **don't just react.** Excuse yourself from the situation as soon as you can, and **get alone with the Lord** (Strategy 60).

† Remember, **you have a real enemy, but it's not your brother or sister.** Ephesians 6:10-12.

† Be **quick to listen, slow to speak and slow to get angry.** James 1:19. Try answering, "So, I hear you saying.... Is that right?" This helps clear up misunderstanding and lowers tension so the person feels heard.

† **No mind-reading.** (Strategy 65) Only God knows what someone is thinking. Instead of assuming evil motives, ask, "When you said ..., did you mean ...?"

† Pray, even while the other person's speaking. **Ask God what He's doing, so you can follow Him there.**

† If you can't see what that is just yet, at least **do the opposite of what the enemy is doing** (Strategy 44).

† **Lay down your opinions and ideas of that person or situation at Jesus' feet, and ask Him for His,** so you can respond through Truth and Love instead of your own strongholds. (Strategy 63)

† **Ask forgiveness.** (Strategy 68) No blaming: "Well, *you* ...!"

† **Forgive.** (Strategies 70-71)

† Try saying under your breath, **"If this is the enemy, in the name of Jesus, stop it!"** (Strategy 85)

† Delay the argument by setting up a meeting at another time, then start that time with prayer, **asking God to lead the conversation.** (See Strategy 81)

† **Hand other people's criticisms of you to the Lord,** so He can show you what is from Him and what is not. (See Strategy 83)

Remember, you can't change that person; that's God's job. But you *can* reduce the conflict, at least within yourself, by seeking God's pathway through it.

> PRAY THROUGH THESE SUGGESTIONS AND ASK THE LORD WHAT NEW HABITS HE WANTS TO FORM IN YOU.

Get alone. Get Truth

1 Peter 5:8-11; Hebrews 12:7-13; 1 Peter 4:12-19

Victory Strategy 60

We often think that because God is loving, He should make everything go our way. But if it didn't work out that way for Jesus, then why do we think it should for us? Mark 14:36, Matthew 10:22-25. Although God often turns things in our favor, **He is more concerned with the condition of your heart than with easing your circumstances.**

So, ***know the condition of your heart. Don't just let your thoughts and emotions rule you.*** Recognize whenever you feel something outside the fruit of the Spirit. Galatians 5:1, 22-25. Then,

† **Excuse yourself from the situation and get alone with Jesus as soon as you can**. Ask Him where that thought or feeling came from, and let Him take you to whatever memory or situation He wants to show you. Then, *feel the lies that took root in your heart through that event, and ask Him for His truth to knock them down.* (Strategy 18)

The more you allow Jesus to heal and cleanse your heart, the closer you'll feel to Him, the louder His voice will sound, the more powerful His Spirit will flow through you, and *the more dangerous you'll be to the enemy.*

Stepping away from conflict isn't easy, however, especially when someone's up in your face pounding in a point. But I find, in about 80 percent of my problems, the real problem is me. Once I've gotten my heart straight with the Lord, there's nothing to fight about with the other person. If God does ask me to confront someone on sin, as in Matthew 18:15, I can do so with His love, compassion and grace, rather than judgment, self-defense, or whatever else ruled me before. Matthew 7:1-5.

Leviticus 19:15; 1 Timothy 5:21

☐ *prejudice*
☐ *partiality*
☐ *favoritism*

Philippians 2:1-16; Leviticus 26:19; Isaiah 16:6

☐ *vanity*
☐ *conceit*
☐ *looking only to my own interests*
☐ *wanting to be served rather than to serve*
☐ *complaining*
☐ *arguing*
☐ *stubbornness*
☐ *pride*
☐ _____
☐ _____

> WHAT ARE SOME OF YOUR NORMAL REACTIONS TO CONFLICT? TALK ABOUT THOSE WITH THE LORD, AND ASK HIM FOR INSTRUCTIONS FOR EACH SPECIFIC SITUATION.

61 Victory Strategy

Truth set-up

Psalm 139:23; Matthew 7:1-5; John 14:16-17

Revelation 2:20-25

- ☐ manipulation
- ☐ control
- ☐ leading others astray
- ☐ tolerating those who lead others astray
- ☐ spiritual abuse
- ☐ twisting Scripture for my own purposes or Satan's
- ☐ convincing others not to obey God
- ☐ dominating
- ☐ possessive
- ☐ placing my will on someone else, rather than seeking God's will together in prayer with that person
- ☐ pushing others into going against their convictions
- ☐ _____
- ☐ _____
- ☐ _____

When a co-worker asked me to help him with a publication, but got angry each time I corrected spelling or grammar, a need to prove myself rose up within me, blowing the top off my Galatians Gauge (Strategy 13).

I said, "Excuse me. I'll be back." Then I went in the other room, and asked the Lord, "Where did *that* come from?" Five years worth of public school memories smashed together into one scene of kids surrounding me to bully and tease me. The lie, "*I must not be important if you treat me this way*," blared in my mind. Then the Lord flashed to a memory of me teaching a little girl without an arm how to draw with her other hand. *My desperate need to be of worth had created in me a false gift of helps.*

Then the Lord flashed back to the picture of mean kids surrounding me; only, this time, I wore a tiara and robe. He said to my heart, **"You were the only royalty in that class. They should have bowed to Who your Father is."**

Suddenly, the need to prove myself vanished. So did that false gift. The next time that man quipped at me, I smiled and said, "I'll be in the other room. If you need anything, let me know."

Now that God has set me free, I no longer need others to accept my help or say nice things to me. *I just love. Because He first loved me.* 1 John 4:19.

Fixing that man's anger issues wasn't my job; it was God's. **I needed to get alone with the Lord so He could heal my own heart.** *Then* He opened the way several days later for my husband and me to help him to freedom through a Truth Encounter. Matthew 7:1-5.

> How was pride involved in my conflict?
>
> Have you ever wanted others to like you or acknowledge you as important? Ask God where that comes from, and let Him show you any memories and associated lies.
>
> Now, ask Him how He sees you.
>
> As you walk through a Truth Encounter (Strategy 18), write in your journal what God shows you.

Truth Counselor

Jeremiah 8:18; Isaiah 9:6; Deuteronomy 32:39; John 8:32

Victory Strategy 62

Before the story in Strategy 61 happened, I already knew I was a daughter of the Most High God, the only Christian in my class. I knew those kids were being mean to me because they didn't have Jesus. So, if I already knew all that truth, why did I react from out of a lie?

It's not enough to know the truth in your head; you need it deep down in your heart to break free.

That's how a rape victim can agree with her counselor that she's not trapped anymore and all men aren't out to get her. But then, only minutes later, she steps into the elevator with a stranger, and ends up in a panicked heap in the corner.

There is only one Healer: God. Not your counselor. Not yoga. Not medication. Not hypnotism or other mind manipulation. The holes in your heart are there for a reason — to be filled with God's love. He is your true Counselor. Jeremiah 8:18.

Whatever problems you have, whatever trials you're going through, they are not just circumstantial. **They are spiritual.** And **the emotions that rage within you are in response to a battle in realms unseen.**

With conventional counseling and medication, you will find helpful coping methods and genuine relief. But **only an encounter with Truth Himself can truly set you free.**

Psalm 42:5
- ☐ heartache, woundedness, pain
- ☐ not feeling loved
- ☐ feeling sorry for myself

1 Corinthians 16:13-14
- ☐ not on alert against the enemy
- ☐ wavering in faith
- ☐ unloving
- ☐ evil thoughts, intentions
- ☐ seeking my own agendas

Mark 5:36
- ☐ unbelief
- ☐ doubt
- ☐ _____

> OPEN YOUR HEART UP WIDE TO THE LORD, LETTING HIM SHOW YOU ANYTHING HE WANTS TO SHOW YOU AND DO ANYTHING HE WANTS TO DO IN YOU.
>
> USE THE GALATIANS GAUGE (STRATEGY 13) AND TRUTH ENCOUNTER STEPS (STRATEGY 18) TO HELP REALIGN YOUR THOUGHTS WITH THE MIND OF CHRIST. WRITE YOUR EXPERIENCES IN YOUR JOURNAL.

63 Victory Strategy: Lay down yours, pick up His

Mark 11:11-17; Proverbs 3:5-7; Isaiah 55:6-9

Matthew 5:20; 7:1-5, James 4:11-12

- ☐ judgment
- ☐ criticism
- ☐ speaking against other Christians
- ☐ legalism (rules over love)
- ☐ not removing my log of judgment before picking at someone's "speck"
- ☐ spiritual pride
- ☐ self-importance
- ☐ placing burdensome expectations on others
- ☐ rejecting, despising those I think don't fit the Christian "ideal"
- ☐ wanting others to look up to me as more spiritual
- ☐ religious spirit
- ☐ giving my advice over seeking God for His

One day, a friend came to my house angry that someone she didn't like had been invited to a gathering she had plans to attend. "She'll *ruin* it!" she raved.

As we worshiped together, I invited her to lay all her opinions and ideas about that woman at Jesus' feet, and ask Him for His: **"Lord, when You look at her, what do You see?"**

As she did that, God showed her all the painful trials the other woman was going through. By the time she left my house, she was smiling with purpose. "I can't wait to see her," she said. "I just want to hug her and tell her how much Jesus and I love her."

From raving anger to joy, love, peace and purpose in just a few minutes. *That's how powerful God's touch is when we seek Him.*

As you can imagine, the gathering she had been so upset about went quite differently than she thought it would. She loved that woman and ministered to her, rather than avoiding her, speaking harshly, or talking behind her back.

† We must get in the habit of laying down all our opinions and ideas of others at Jesus' feet, so we can **seek His viewpoint** and break free from the judgment and other thought-traps the enemy sets to ensnare us into thinking and doing his will.

> WHAT OPINIONS AND IDEAS DO YOU NEED TO LAY DOWN BEFORE THE LORD? SPEND TIME IN WORSHIP, AND ASK HIM, "LORD, WHEN YOU LOOK AT _____, WHAT DO YOU SEE?"
>
> HOW DOES HIS VIEWPOINT CHANGE THE WAY YOU FEEL AND RESPOND? JOURNAL YOUR ANSWER.

Fight for your brother

James 1:19-20; Proverbs 18:13

Victory Strategy 64

Misunderstandings are one of the enemy's favorite tactics for dividing relationships. If he can plant thoughts in your mind about hidden motives or meanings behind what someone says, then he has tricked you into obeying his lead, rather than the Spirit's.

So, when your friend is sharing her heart, don't spend that time formulating your argument. *Listen* to her.

† Be **quick to listen, slow to speak, and slow to get angry.** James 1:19.

One time, God urged me to apologize to my husband about something. Not wanting any misunderstanding, I sought the Lord for the precise words, and then waited until the kids were in bed to invite him to sit on the couch and talk with me.

When I said the prepared apology (which was sweet, by the way), his reaction was so adverse, I actually stopped him. "What do you think I just said?" I asked.

He quoted to me a sentence that *rhymed word-for-word*, but was an *accusation* rather than an apology!

We were sitting so close to each other, he couldn't have misheard me. *The enemy had twisted my words in the air!*

The next few minutes we spent in prayer together, rebuking a spirit of misunderstanding, telling the enemy to go, and inviting Jesus to fill our home with His presence.

Remember, *you have a real enemy, but it's not your brother.* **Fight *for* him, not *against*,** *and join hands in a united front against your true enemy, Satan.*

Mt. 5, 7; Jas. 4 ...
- [ ] preventing God's people from serving Him because of gender, education, or qualifications I feel they lack

1 John 4:7-21
- [ ] inability to love
- [ ] not letting God's love change me
- [ ] not letting God's love flow through me to others
- [ ] _____
- [ ] _____
- [ ] _____

ARE YOU QUICK TO LISTEN, SLOW TO SPEAK, AND SLOW TO GET ANGRY?

HAS SATAN BEEN ALLOWED TO INSTIGATE MISUNDERSTANDINGS AND ACCUSATIONS IN YOUR RELATIONSHIPS? WHAT IS THE LORD ASKING YOU TO DO ABOUT THAT? ASK HIM.

Victory Strategy 65

No mind-reading

Exodus 20:16; James 4:11-12; Matthew 7:1-5; 22:37-40

James 1:19-25
- ☐ quick to anger
- ☐ short tempered
- ☐ easily agitated
- ☐ verbal attacks
- ☐ slow to listen
- ☐ jumping to conclusions
- ☐ quick to speak
- ☐ excessive talking
- ☐ interrupting
- ☐ talking over others
- ☐ pushing my point
- ☐ knowing what the Word says, but then ignoring it to do whatever I feel like doing

Ephesians 4:31-32; Matthew 5:21-22
- ☐ bitterness
- ☐ unforgiveness
- ☐ rage
- ☐ anger
- ☐ brawling
- ☐ _____

I praise God for a husband who listens to me and fights for me. But the truth is I have lost several close friends to mind-reading. Unlike my husband, they were unwilling to hear the truth or fight together with me against the real enemy.

Mind-reading happens when we *imagine negative thoughts or evil motives behind others' words, expressions, or actions; and then treat them as if our imaginations are true.*

A mind-reader is in serious trouble because of James 4:11-12 and Matthew 7:1-5. Only God knows our thoughts and motives. He alone is our Judge. And *He didn't die and give you His job!* So if you're not seeking Him for His viewpoint (Strategy 63) and you're not listening to the person you're mind-reading, then *whose voice are you listening to?* John 8:42-47; 10:10. _____

† **Mind-reading is a form of divination.** *Get rid of it!*

When you listen to Satan instead of Love, tearing people down with lies, you're welcoming the enemy's leadership in your life over the Holy Spirit's.

Not only that, but the Bible pronounces a myriad of curses on those who falsely accuse and otherwise persecute God's people. (See Strategy 72.)

† **Before you accuse, make sure you know the facts.** Ask questions like, "When you said…, did you mean…?"

If they don't answer truthfully, that's between them and God. Your job is to listen. James 1:19. And to *love.* Matthew 22:37-40.

> HAVE YOU BEEN MIND-READING OTHERS?
> DO YOU CONTINUE TO BELIEVE YOUR ASSUMPTIONS ARE TRUE, EVEN WHEN THAT PERSON TELLS YOU OTHERWISE?
> ASK THE LORD, AND JOURNAL WHAT HE SHOWS YOU.
> SEEK HIM FOR A TRUTH ENCOUNTER (STRATEGY 18) IF HE LEADS YOU TO, AND ASK FORGIVENESS OF ANYONE YOU'VE SINNED AGAINST.

Change me first

John 10:1-27; Jeremiah 50:7; Romans 12:1-3

Victory Strategy 66

Can you see how important it is to fear the Lord? To not lean on your own understanding, but seek Him in everything? Proverbs 3:5-7, 2 Corinthians 10:3-5.

Love takes the pressure off. You don't have to be the judge of someone's character, or fix everything you think is wrong with that person. That's not your job.

Your job is your own heart. And to love. Matthew 22:37-40.

The best way to help others walk the right way is to walk that way yourself.

Love. Spread wide the carpet of grace. Forgive. Speak truth. Pray. Obey the Lord. And know that, if you've done those things, *it is Christ in you they are rejecting*, not you.

If you've messed up, no matter how bad that mess seems right now, He can bring the good out of it. Just ask forgiveness of whomever you need to, and fix your heart on Jesus. Let Him heal your wounds, expose the strongholds in you through this trial, tear them down, and set you free.

As others see the Good Shepherd carry you, as they watch you feasting on the sweet, green pastures of His presence and love, **they just might hate the bitter weeds they've been sucking on out there around the fringes of the flock where lions lie in wait, and turn to Jesus.**

So, intercede for those who hurt you and speak truth as God asks you to (Matthew 18:15), but lift the burden of that person's problems off your shoulders, and hand it to Jesus. He's strong enough to carry your load and your friend's load too.

If you let Him change your own heart first, you're likely to see a change in your friend, as well.

Lamentations 3:46-66, Psalm 73:7-8

- ☐ *imaginations against someone*
- ☐ *false accusations*
- ☐ *attacking those who are innocent*
- ☐ *mind-reading hidden motives behind someone's words and treating them as if it's truth*

Job 5:2, 36:13; Leviticus 19:18

- ☐ *holding grudges*
- ☐ *seeking revenge*
- ☐ *resentment*
- ☐ *retaliation*
- ☐ *back-biting*

WHAT'S WEIGHING YOU DOWN? HAND IT TO THE LORD. DON'T SPEND ALL YOUR ENERGY FOCUSING ON WHAT THAT OTHER PERSON NEEDS CHANGED. **LET GOD CHANGE YOU FIRST.** THEN WATCH AND SEE WHAT HE WILL DO WITH YOUR FRIEND, AND BE OPEN FOR HIM TO USE YOU.

67 Victory Strategy: The Matthew 18:15 Principle

Matthew 7:1-5; 18:15-20; Ephesians 4:15

Proverbs 13:10

- ☐ causing strife
- ☐ not taking advice
- ☐ starting arguments
- ☐ attacking or oppressing others
- ☐ pursuing others to pull them into an argument
- ☐ repeating my point over and over without giving others room to speak
- ☐ _____

Galatians 5:16-21

- ☐ impurity
- ☐ hatred
- ☐ discord
- ☐ jealousy
- ☐ fits of rage
- ☐ selfish ambition
- ☐ dissension
- ☐ controversy
- ☐ contention
- ☐ factions or clicks
- ☐ drunkenness
- ☐ partying
- ☐ orgies

One way the enemy gets us to do his dirty work is through saying bad things about others, rather than letting God transform our own hearts or lovingly confronting.

Most of the problems we have with others really are our own. If I seek God for freedom from whatever heart issue distresses me, and let Him topple my lies with His truth, seldom is there ever anything to confront the other person on. Because the conflict is gone, at least within me.

But there are times when that person's sinful habits hurt the body of Christ and need to be confronted. Jesus' words in Matthew 18:15-17 provide us with a guide for this:

1. **Don't talk behind someone's back.** If you have a problem with that person, go to her personally.
2. **Make sure what you're confronting her on is sin**, not just something you don't like about her or disagree with.
3. **Speak the truth in love.**

   1) **Clean your own heart** out first. (See Strategy 63)

   2) **Make sure no judgment clouds your view.** Matthew 7:1-5.

   3) **Lay down all your opinions about her, and ask Jesus for His.**

   4) Set up a time to meet with her, and start that time with **prayer, asking God to lead.**

   5) **Speak the truth in love.** Ephesians 4:15. Be prepared with Scripture to encourage. Ask questions that will help her share her heart, so you can listen well. Pray for her. Matthew 18:18-20.

4. **If she listens, then you have your sister back. But if she doesn't, go and find others** she respects, a friend who also has been affected by the situation, a counselor, or someone else God leads you to, and meet with her again together with that person.

> IS THERE SOMEONE YOU NEED TO CONFRONT ON SIN? ASK THE LORD. AND THEN FOLLOW THESE STEPS AND ANYTHING ELSE GOD LEADS YOU TO DO.

Humbly ask forgiveness

1 John 1:5-9; Psalm 139:23-24

Victory Strategy 68

Remember, pride is at the heart of every argument. *Make sure it's not yours.*

Humility draws God near, and a contrite heart is the quickest way to His favor and protection. *Humility is also the quickest way to joy and peace,* because you get to watch God fulfill His purposes in your trial.

So, it's important in any conflict to

† Ask the Lord what part you have played in the problem, and **be quick to ask forgiveness.**

Humbly asking forgiveness should stir the other person's heart to do the same, but the truth is *that seldom happens,* even among Christians. I have found, in most situations, proud, angry people just get all the angrier and haughtier when I apologize: "See, I *was* right! *You....*"

So, **don't use apologies as a manipulative means to get the other person to back down.** Just, simply, **are you in sin?** Then ask forgiveness.

If others puff up all the more, that is between them and God. *Don't stress over trying to fix someone else's attitude.* **Only say what God leads you to say, and leave the other person's heart up to the Lord.**

1 John 1:8-10; Matthew 18:15

- ☐ not listening when confronted on sin
- ☐ denying wrongdoing
- ☐ argumentative
- ☐ defensive
- ☐ not caring about those I've hurt
- ☐ persisting in conflict
- ☐ talking behind others' backs rather than speaking to the one who sinned against me
- ☐ ignoring conflict
- ☐ not being honest about sin
- ☐ _____

> IS THERE ANYTHING YOU NEED TO ASK SOMEONE FORGIVENESS FOR? ASK THE LORD, AND THEN LET HIM LEAD YOU INTO THAT ENCOUNTER. REMEMBER, DON'T WORRY ABOUT THE OTHER PERSON'S RESPONSE. YOU ARE ONLY RESPONSIBLE FOR YOUR OWN HEART BEFORE GOD AND THAT OTHER PERSON. LOVE GOD, LOVE OTHERS, AND MOVE ON IN FREEDOM. MATTHEW 22:37-40.

69 Victory Strategy

Do everything in love

John 8:32; Matthew 22:37-40; Romans 8:31-39; 1 John 4:8

Colossians 3:18-25; Ephesians 5:22-6:2; Hebrews 13:17; 1 Timothy 2:1-4

☐ not honoring and reverencing husband
☐ not submitting to husband, parents or other authority
☐ dishonoring husband, parents or other authority
☐ rebellion
☐ procrastination
☐ mocking, slander or bitterness toward authority, rather than praying for them and blessing them
☐ frigidity
☐ _____
☐ _____

Romans 13:8

☐ incurred debts
☐ not returning money borrowed from a friend

The issues we have with others are most often rooted in our own issues; and until we get those straight with God, we will continue to experience the same recurring relationship problems.

That's why it's so important to duck out of a stressful situation as fast as you can and get alone with Jesus, so you can ask Him why you feel the way you do *before* you respond to that person from out of your junk.

Notice what the enemy's trying to do and purpose to do the opposite. *Look for what God's doing and join Him there.* Matthew 22:37-40 is a great guide for finding God's will, no matter the situation.

One thing God is always doing in every situation is *drawing you closer to Himself*. So, get a head start on that. James 4:8a. If people are around and you need to get alone with Jesus right away, head for the bathroom and lock the door. You don't have to spend three hours in there. A Truth Encounter (Strategy 18) usually only takes a few minutes. But it is crucial that you learn to recognize the enemy's assaults and do whatever you need to do to let Truth set you free, so you can get back to that main assignment God's given you that makes Satan so afraid: *LOVE*.

You see, **love not only defeats Satan's plans, it defeats him.** Romans 8:31-39. **Love is the greatest power. When you stand in Christ's love to love others, you have won the battle.** And Satan knows it. That's why he works so hard to get you all upset that things aren't going your way — so you'll pout, or get mad, or force someone to do what you want, or *anything other than walking in that first fruit of the Spirit*. Galatians 5:22a.

> IN WHAT WAYS HAVE YOU RESPONDED LATELY OUTSIDE OF LOVE'S EMPOWERING? 1 JOHN 4:8. HOW CAN LOVE CHANGE THAT SITUATION?

Forgive

Matthew 6:14-15; Psalm 32:1-5; Romans 12:17-21

Victory Strategy 70

When Jesus died on the cross, He paid for *all* your sin — from the tiniest infraction to that monstrous mistake you still regret. So, if your mile-high debt has been forgiven entirely, why are you stressing over someone else's minuscule speck? Matthew 7:1-5, 18:21-35.

Unforgiveness is not only spiritually detrimental because of Matthew 6:15; it is also physically, emotionally, and mentally dangerous. Psalm 32:1-5. In fact, most cases of depression, suicidal thoughts, and stress-related physical pain can be traced back to an event or series of events where unforgiveness led to bitterness and other sicknesses of the soul. **No amount of medication can fix that.**

No matter how you try to "punish" that hurtful person with your ugly thoughts and words, you can't change him anyway. Only God can do that. But **you *can* change how his sin affects you.** *Let God empower you to forgive.*

Forgiveness is not saying that what the offender did is okay. *Sin is never okay.* And it's not forgetting, although forgetting sometimes happens as a result of forgiveness.

- **Forgiveness is cutting the tie that binds your heart to someone else's offense so the enemy can't jerk you around by it anymore.**
- **Forgiveness is a choice.** *Keep choosing forgiveness, and your feelings will eventually follow.*
- **Forgiveness relinquishes vengeance into God's hands to be dealt with by Him** so you can get back to shining His light and enjoying the grace, love, peace, joy, and freedom you were created for. Romans 12:19, Galatians 5:22-23.

Luke 17:1-2
- ☐ child abuse — verbal, emotional, physical, sexual, spiritual or otherwise
- ☐ leading others to sin
- ☐ causing others to stumble
- ☐ blocking children from coming to God

Ephesians 6:4
- ☐ not disciplining my children
- ☐ provoking my children to anger, making them lose heart
- ☐ not training them up in the Lord

> Ask the Lord, "Is there anyone I haven't forgiven?" If a memory comes to mind, walk through the steps in the next strategy.

71 Victory Strategy — Freedom through forgiveness

Mark 11:25, Romans 4:7; 12:14; Colossians 3:13; 1 Peter 4:8

Job 22:4-11, 42:7

- [ ] false accusations
- [ ] imagining sin in people and treating them as if it's true
- [ ] not believing what others say
- [ ] not believing the best about someone
- [ ] forming opinions of others based on slander or imaginations rather than facts and God's viewpoint
- [ ] causing misunderstandings
- [ ] doing and saying what the enemy leads me to, rather than seeking God
- [ ] believing and speaking lies
- [ ] prophesying false words over others
- [ ] speaking for God when God hasn't asked me to speak

1. If an offense against you (whether past or present) brings up anger or hurt, get alone with the Lord and ask Him where those feelings come from. Let Him take you anywhere and show you anything He wants to (even if it's another memory).

2. As you sit there with the Lord, allow yourself to remember together with Him the event He brings to mind. Feel what you felt when it happened, so you can recognize the lies the enemy planted.

3. Then, from the midst of that memory and all the thoughts and feelings that accompany it, **choose to forgive.** [I've found it especially powerful to say it aloud: "I forgive you, _____ (name), for _____ (offense)."]

4. **Intercede** (Strategy 72), asking God's forgiveness and mercy for both you and your offender, and **bless him**. "Lord, please forgive me for my anger and bitterness. And please forgive (person) and have mercy on him. Set him free from _____, and draw him to Yourself.... In the name of Jesus, I bless (person) with (grace, peace, a closer relationship with Christ, etc.)."

5. If the memory God brought you to is not the initial event in #1 that was bothering you, check and see if that first one is healed now. If not, go through steps 1-4 for that memory.

6. If any of those memories return, use them as a reminder. "I forgive (person), and I bless (person) in Jesus' name...." If you pray all the more for others' salvation and freedom each time the enemy brings that offense to mind, **he will lose more ground by reminding you** than not. *Eventually, he'll stop.*

7. If you still have anger, pain, or other negative emotions regarding an event, follow the Truth Encounter steps (Strategy 18), or between steps 2 and 3 on this page, ask the Lord, "Where were You when that happened? What were You doing or saying?" Look around for Him in your memory and listen for His truth.

> FOLLOW THESE STEPS IN YOUR QUIET TIME TODAY, AND WRITE YOUR EXPERIENCE IN YOUR JOURNAL.

Plead for mercy

Psalm 35; 109; Luke 23:34

Victory Strategy 72

Proverbs 10:4; Hebrews 6:12
- ☐ laziness
- ☐ spiritual laziness
- ☐ no initiative
- ☐ knowing what I need to do but not doing it
- ☐ putting off obedience until I "feel like it"
- ☐ feeling overwhelmed at the thought of hard work
- ☐ simple-minded
- ☐ seeking the easy way out
- ☐ making others do my chores
- ☐ _____
- ☐ _____

When my best friends launched an assault of false accusations against me that went on for months, even years, their relentless attacks caused excruciating pain. But Christ had loved me in all my messes and forgiven me of so much, how could I not also forgive them?

Still, as the attacks went on, I continued daily in the Word, seeking God's instructions for every battle. He highlighted in Scripture all the many, various curses that fall upon those who falsely accuse and attack God's people. By the time I got to Psalm 109, I literally trembled with fear of the Lord. *Were all those terrible things going to happen to these women I loved?*

Then the Lord moved me to Luke 23:34, where Jesus said, "Father, forgive them, for they do not know what they are doing."

Jesus didn't just forgive. *He interceded for His persecutors. He knew the curses that would fall on them and He stood in the gap, asking for His Father to have mercy and forgive them.*

Once I realized how much danger my friends were in, I stopped focusing so much on my own suffering, and began interceding for their deliverance.

Years later, one of the women, who had experienced panic attacks and demonic visitations, shared with me that God had set her free from some of her issues. *She even asked my forgiveness.*

† As you forgive those who persecute you, **intercede for them** as well, asking for God's mercy on them to forgive them and set them free.

> HAS ANYONE FALSELY ACCUSED YOU OR PERSECUTED YOU IN OTHER WAYS? SPEND SOME TIME INTERCEDING FOR THEM TODAY (STEP 4 IN STRATEGY 71).

73 Victory strategy

Curses turned blessings

Deuteronomy 23:5, Psalm 109:28; Deuteronomy 28

Romans 1:18-32

- ☐ suppressing truth
- ☐ not glorifying God
- ☐ ungrateful
- ☐ foolish
- ☐ exchanging truth for lies
- ☐ lustful
- ☐ homosexual thoughts or actions
- ☐ indecent acts
- ☐ perverse
- ☐ depraved mind
- ☐ evil
- ☐ strife
- ☐ gossip
- ☐ senseless
- ☐ faithless
- ☐ hatred of God
- ☐ insolent
- ☐ boastful
- ☐ heartless
- ☐ ruthless
- ☐ willful
- ☐ disobedient to God
- ☐ _____

Proverbs 10:17

- ☐ not heeding discipline
- ☐ ignoring correction
- ☐ _____

Obeying the Lord places us in His favor and under His protection. In fact, when we love God and obey His commands, He often transforms curses into blessings.

I know my former friends didn't mean to curse, but their false accusations ("You're mean!" "You have a demon!" "God wants you to choose vengeance, not mercy!" "You don't worship!" "You don't pray!" "Jesus lied!") could have fallen that way if my Shield had let them.

Without any context for their attacks, and with no reply to my questions, all I could do was take each of their accusations into my quiet times with the Lord and let Him sift through them, cleaning out my heart and showing me His viewpoint. Then I let Him guide me to reply to their letters through His love rather than through my hurt.

One morning, two of them wrote me separate letters, saying, "How come you always come out on top?" I didn't know what they meant. I felt more like mud trampled under stomping feet than someone on top of it all. So, I just handed those letters over to Jesus, just like all the others, and went about my day.

That night, as I crawled into bed and opened my Bible for a "goodnight kiss," I just "happened" to be in Deuteronomy 28, where God gives His people the choice of blessings or curses. Verse 13 says, "The Lord will make you the head, not the tail. If you pay attention to the commands of the Lord your God that I give you this day and carefully follow them, **you will always be at the top, never at the bottom**."

What? *How did He orchestrate their letters to arrive on the very day I was to read that passage?* He is so ... God.

Now, that truth is sealed in my heart. Forever.

ASK GOD TO BE A SHIELD AROUND YOU, TO CANCEL EVERY CURSE AND TURN IT INTO A BLESSING INSTEAD.

Break off curses

Job 31:30; Psalm 59:12; Galatians 1:10; Hebrews 12:1-3

Victory Strategy 74

Negative words can fall like curses, whether we mean them to or not.

A child whose parent said to her in the heat of anger, "You can't do anything right," may find, sure enough, she can't seem to excel in school, jobs, relationships, etc.

If a kid in elementary school said to you, "You're fat!" or "You're stupid!" those words may ring in your ears each time you step on the scales or fail at something.

Or maybe you've said those things about yourself.

Either way, **negative confessions contrary to Truth and who you are in Christ carry power in the spiritual realm,** *because agreeing with the father of lies is disagreeing with Jesus.* John 8:42-47.

To break curses and invite God's blessings and covering, try praying something like this:

"In the name of Jesus, I cut off from myself the words, "_____," and any negative effects or curses that may have fallen upon me or my children because of them. I break that curse and any others in the name of Jesus, and declare that I belong to Jesus and I am Who He says I am. I am _____ (what the Word says about you that is opposite what that curse said). In the name of Jesus, I forbid the enemy to pick on me, my children, or my children's children ever again with regard to that now broken curse. I declare God's _____ (Kingdom Culture qualities that are opposite what the enemy says about you, like the fruit of the Spirit) over me, my children, and their children for all generations in the name of Jesus...."

Romans 1:16
- ☐ ashamed of Christ, won't talk about Him with others
- ☐ afraid to witness
- ☐ afraid of what others think of my Christianity
- ☐ afraid to pray in public
- ☐ intimidated by those against Christ
- ☐ _____

Titus 2:11
- ☐ can't say "no"
- ☐ ungodliness
- ☐ giving in to wordly passions
- ☐ lack of self-control

> HAS ANYONE SPOKEN OVER YOU SOMETHING NEGATIVE CONTRARY TO GOD'S WORD OR TO WHO YOU ARE IN CHRIST? BREAK OFF THOSE WORDS NOW, USING A PRAYER LIKE THE ONE ABOVE.
>
> WALK THROUGH A TRUTH ENCOUNTER (STRATEGY 18), IF GOD LEADS, SO HE CAN HEAL YOU AND SET YOU FREE TO BE ALL HE CREATED YOU TO BE.

Victory Strategy 75: Know and live your purpose

Psalm 139:13-16; Isaiah 42:5-6; 43:7, 10, 21; 44:2, 8, 21; 46:4, 10

James 5
- ☐ not paying workers
- ☐ not paying fair wages
- ☐ hoarding
- ☐ not helping those in need
- ☐ stingy
- ☐ unhospitable
- ☐ using others
- ☐ grumbling
- ☐ negative
- ☐ swearing
- ☐ impure vows
- ☐ breaking promises
- ☐ not following through on commitments
- ☐ not worshipping
- ☐ not helping others turn from sin

Jeremiah 30:15
- ☐ self-pity

Proverbs 1:22; 3:34
- ☐ mocking
- ☐ scoffing
- ☐ sarcasm
- ☐ insults
- ☐ teasing
- ☐ belittling
- ☐ hurtful comments

Hurt people hurt people. But there's also another reason the enemy wants to tear you down through others.

There is only one you. No one else has the same experiences, thoughts, looks, abilities, gifts, or journey with God that you have. In fact, before you were born, when God thought you up and formed you in your mother's womb, He already appointed for you a special assignment — a unique way He would shine His light through you that no one else would be able to do quite the same.

But whether you know and walk in that purpose yet or not, **the enemy knows.** In fact, **he has been working day and night to tell you that you are the opposite.**

That's why someone God has crafted for Christian leadership feels like a failure each time she leads. "Others criticize me, and no one's following, anyway. I just want to give up, do something normal people do...."

That's why a bubbly young woman who draws so many people into Jesus through her love and joy has been accused of being weird or fake so many times that her smile has faded and she seldom speaks of Jesus anymore.

Don't let the enemy do that to you! **Find out God's purposes for your life, use all your gifts for His glory, know what He says about you, and *live* it.**

---

1. WHAT DIFFICULT CIRCUMSTANCES MOST OFTEN KNOCK YOU DOWN? WHAT CRITICISMS HURT YOU MOST? WHAT NEGATIVE THOUGHTS ABOUT YOURSELF MOST OFTEN RUN THROUGH YOUR MIND? *IT'S POSSIBLE GOD CREATED YOU THE EXACT OPPOSITE!*

2. HOW DOES GOD USE YOU MOST TO DRAW OTHERS CLOSER TO HIM? WHAT ARE YOUR PASSIONS? WHAT BRINGS YOU JOY? WHAT GIFTS HAVE OTHERS SEEN IN YOU AND ENCOURAGED YOU TO PURSUE? *ASK PEOPLE YOU TRUST HOW THEY SEE GOD USING YOU.*

3. ASK THE LORD TO SHOW YOU YOUR UNIQUE ASSIGNMENT(S) HE CRAFTED YOU FOR. JOURNAL WHAT HE SHOWS YOU AND STEP OUT TO FULFILL HIS PURPOSES FOR YOU IN HIS EMPOWERING. **PURPOSE TO BE THE OPPOSITE OF WHO THE ENEMY SAYS YOU ARE.**

Speak blessings, not curses

Victory Strategy 76

James 3:9; Genesis 12:3; Leviticus 20:9; Job 31:30

Sometimes negative confessions don't come from someone else but from ourselves. Have you ever said something against yourself, like, "I'm fat," "My hips are big," "I'm dying of hunger," "I'm just like my mom," "I'll never be able to do that"?

What if the enemy is using your words as an invitation for him to carry out his purposes in your life? What if he wants you to continually struggle with your weight, ... to have pain in your hips and legs, ... to have near-death experiences, ... to go through the same problems, strongholds, failures, and illnesses your mother has, ... to fail over and over again, no matter how hard you try...?

I don't fully understand all that goes on in the spiritual realm, and probably won't until I get to Heaven. But I choose now, while I'm here on this earth, to speak positive confessions over myself, circumstances, and others. To speak what God is saying. To know the truth and live it.

I figure I have enough battles to fight as it is without inviting more. **If words have power, then I want to use mine to open up channels for God's blessings to flow in my life and in the lives of those around me.**

Job 31:30; Psalm 59:12
- [ ] cursing ourselves or others with our negative words and attitudes

Matthew 12:38-39
- [ ] seeking after signs
- [ ] emotionalism
- [ ] striving for miracles
- [ ] discouraged when miracles don't happen
- [ ] loss of faith when I don't see God do what I want Him to
- [ ] _____

HAVE YOU EVER SAID SOMETHING NEGATIVE ABOUT YOURSELF OR SOMEONE ELSE? ARE YOU IN THE HABIT OF USING PHRASES LIKE, "I'M DYING OF ..." OR "I CAN'T ...," OR "I'M NOT ...," OR ANYTHING ELSE NEGATIVE GOD IS REMINDING YOU OF — WORDS THAT DO NOT EXPRESS WHAT HE SAYS IS TRUE?

TAKE A MOMENT TO ASK THE LORD IF THERE ARE ANY CURSES YOU'VE SPOKEN OVER YOURSELF OR OTHERS THAT HE WANTS YOU TO RENOUNCE AND CUT OFF, AND FOLLOW THE PRAYER IN STRATEGY 74.

NOW PRAY FOR YOURSELF OR THAT OTHER PERSON THE OPPOSITE, KINGDOM QUALITIES AS BLESSINGS.

77 Victory Strategy

Guard your mouth!

Ecclesiastes 3:1, 7; 5:2; Proverbs 21:23

Exodus 20:1-21; Matthew 15:19; Romans 1:25

☐ *disbelieving God (miracles, the Word, etc.)*
☐ *critical toward God*
☐ *false religions*
☐ *idolatry*
☐ *worshipping other gods*
☐ *intellectualism*
☐ *worship of money*
☐ *worship of entertainment*
☐ *worship of people*
☐ *worship of work*
☐ *not putting God first in my life*
☐ *not setting aside time to be with God daily*
☐ *exchanging the truth of God for a lie*
☐ *taking the Lord's name in vain*
☐ *misusing God's name*
☐ *lying about God*

There is a time to speak, but here are some **times to be silent, lest the enemy speak through you**:

- When you haven't listened yet. James 1:19.
- When your words destroy rather than bring life. John 10:10.
- When you're angry. James 1:19-20.
- When you can't say anything nice. James 3:9, Proverbs 25:28, Proverbs 16:27, Matthew 18:15-17.
- When it's a lie or a mind-read. Exodus 20:16.
- When you're just repeating what someone else said, but you haven't checked to make sure it's true. Proverbs 18:13, Deuteronomy 17:6.
- When it's judgment, gossip, or slander. James 4:11-12.
- When your words might bring a weaker brother down. 1 Corinthians 8:1-11.
- When you diminish God's holiness, greatness, grace, love or other aspect of His character. Ecclesiastes 5:2.
- If you've said it more than once, and now you're just nagging. Proverbs 19:13.

Proverbs 21:23: *"Those who guard their mouths and their tongues keep themselves from calamity."*

> HAVE YOU SPOKEN WHEN YOU SHOULD HAVE BEEN SILENT? ASK THE LORD AND LOOK OVER THE LIST ABOVE. ARE THERE OTHER TIMES GOD HAS ASKED YOU TO CLOSE YOUR MOUTH? JOURNAL WHAT HE SHOWS YOU, AND YOUR REPENTANCE.

Eternal mindset

2 Corinthians 4:16-18; Matthew 6:19-21

Victory strategy 78

If you want to defeat your enemy's plans for you, then take on an eternal mindset.

We are merely strangers, after all, passing through earth on our way to our real home in Heaven. We're not here to get comfortable or to make sure everyone likes us.

What we do with the brief time we have here on earth has everything to do with how we will experience eternity. In fact, the Bible speaks repeatedly about the importance of storing up treasures in Heaven.

But when this messy world is up in our face, it's hard to think about eternal things. Even something as small as a headache can take precedence over being loving and kind.

But a headache is temporal. It's a very real pain I have to go through right now, but it's not going to follow me to Heaven.

If I yell at my kids in my pain, even that sin is temporary because of what Jesus did for me. It's not who I am in Christ. It's just something to throw off, so I can run faster toward the One Who is eternal. Hebrews 12:1-3.

But if I stop, SEE my kids, ask their forgiveness, and LOVE them, I've just stepped into the eternal.

Because **love is eternal**. 1 Corinthians 13:13.

And so is repentance. 1 John 1:8-10, Psalm 103:12.

When my heart is humble and broken over my sin down here on earth, in Heaven my slate is wiped clean.

Let's run this race such that when we get to Heaven and the book of our life is opened, all that is written on the pages is how we loved. Matthew 22:37-40.

Ex. 20:1-21; Matt. 15:19; Rom. 1:25 ...

- ☐ misrepresenting God
- ☐ not setting aside a time of rest
- ☐ not setting aside a day for the Lord
- ☐ unloving toward parents, not caring for their needs
- ☐ rebellious toward parents
- ☐ murder
- ☐ murderous thoughts
- ☐ saying, "I'm going to kill you!" "I hope you die!" "I'm dying of ...," or other death talk

> WHAT ARE SOME ACTIVITIES OR SITUATIONS IN WHICH YOU FIND IT PARTICULARLY DIFFICULT TO FIX YOUR MIND ON ETERNAL THINGS? ASK THE LORD FOR A PLAN. WRITE IN YOUR JOURNAL WHAT HE SHOWS YOU AND PURPOSE TO WALK IT OUT IN REAL LIFE.

79 Victory Strategy

From mundane to mighty

2 Corinthians 4:5-18; Matthew 6:19-21

Ex. 20:1-21;
Matt. 15:19;
Rom. 1:25 ...

- ☐ suicidal thoughts
- ☐ death wishes
- ☐ abortion
- ☐ adultery
- ☐ infidelity
- ☐ stealing, theft
- ☐ dishonesty
- ☐ kleptomania
- ☐ stealing information
- ☐ shoplifting
- ☐ borrowing something and never returning it
- ☐ walking off with something that's not mine
- ☐ false testimony
- ☐ lying
- ☐ assigning evil motives to others' comments or glances; then treating them as if my imaginations are true)
- ☐ swayed by desire
- ☐ gullible
- ☐ foolish
- ☐ _____
- ☐ _____

What does it look like to fix our eyes on eternal things when this world is all up in our face? When that long line just got longer because THAT MAN JUST CUT IN FRONT OF ME? When traffic is jammed? When all four kids disobey at the same time? When the air conditioner breaks and it's the hottest day of the year? When things just are *so* not going my way?

Love. That's what it looks like. Because love is eternal. 1 Corinthians 13:13.

When my heart is fixed on eternal things, a long line becomes an opportunity to pray for the people around me. Yes, even that man who just cut in line. What if no one has ever prayed for him in his life? What if God pushed him in front of me just for that purpose? What if he needs Jesus, and that long line will give me just enough time to share the Gospel with him?

I can sit in traffic and get angry that I'll be late for work, or I can go on an adventure with the Lord, ask Him about the people in the cars around me, pray for their needs one by one. I can worship, letting the Lord turn a mundane situation into a God-awesome one, with Heaven meeting earth right there where the rubber hits the road.

I can yell at my kids when they disobey, or I can stop, pray, and ask God what to do. Right there in front of them. So they see me, see the way He calms me down and changes me, see the way He individually deals with each of them according to their own issues and needs.

And what if that repairman who comes to fix my air conditioner needs Jesus?

When things don't go my way, it's just one more chance to draw closer to the Lord, make a difference in this world, and build up a pile of riches in Heaven. 2 Corinthians 4:5-18. *Where it counts.* Matthew 6:19-21.

> WHAT ARE SOME WAYS YOU CAN CHANGE MUNDANE MOMENTS INTO GOD-AWESOME ONES THIS WEEK? ASK GOD, OBEY, AND JOURNAL YOUR EXPERIENCE.

Expect God

Isaiah 40:31; Psalm 37; 87:7

Victory Strategy 80

Ex. 20:1-21; Matt. 15:19; Rom. 1:25 ...

☐ hanging out with those involved in unholy acts, letting them influence me, rather than me influencing them to draw near to God
☐ easily seduced
☐ letting people take wrong advantage of me
☐ tempting others to sin
☐ flirtatious
☐ seeking men's love
☐ sexual perversion

One of the main tactics the enemy uses to frustrate us is failed expectations.

When people don't follow through on their promises, or don't react the way we want or expect them to, we feel angry, hurt, betrayed.

And when things don't turn out the way we expected, especially if we prayed and thought we had enough faith for that, we feel discouraged, hopeless, angry at God....

But people are imperfect, and we live in a fallen world where things often go wrong. We have a real enemy who knows exactly what you're expecting and purposefully twists situations to mess with your heart, divide relationships, and make you doubt the God Who loves you.

We need to take our focus off of what we expect others to do, what we expect to happen, and *even what we expect God to do*. **God is not a toy machine — insert the right prayer, and out pops what you want. He is Holy, Mighty, Sovereign, Perfect, and** *He is doing many things you can't see right now.*

So just drop your expectations of everything and everyone, and **expect God**. Because **God is always happening**. He's always ready to meet you right here where you are and turn your frustrating moment into a God-awesome moment filled with love, joy, peace, power, and even miracles.

From the very start of your problem to the very end, His desire has been to deepen your relationship with Him. The sooner you look to God and let Him be the fulfillment of all your desires, the sooner this whole situation will turn around into something good. Psalm 37:4, Romans 8:28.

HAVE YOU FELT FRUSTRATED LATELY?
WHAT WERE YOU EXPECTING THAT DIDN'T HAPPEN?
HAND YOUR THOUGHTS OVER TO JESUS AND INVITE HIM TO DO WHATEVER HE WANTS.
EXPECT HIM TO SURPRISE YOU WITH HIMSELF.
WRITE IN YOUR JOURNAL WHAT HE SAYS OR DOES.

81 Victory Strategy: Let God lead the conversation

Proverbs 3:5-7; Isaiah 1:18; Colossians 3:12-14

Ex. 20:1-21; Matt. 15:19; Rom. 1:25 ...

- ☐ dressing inappropriately (showing a lot of skin, cleavage, see-through clothes, short shorts, tight clothes, bikini, etc.)
- ☐ homosexuality
- ☐ lesbian thoughts
- ☐ necrophilia
- ☐ nymphomania
- ☐ lust
- ☐ masturbation
- ☐ sadomasochism (S&M)
- ☐ child molestation
- ☐ fornication
- ☐ incest
- ☐ rape
- ☐ sodomy
- ☐ fantasy
- ☐ illicit sex
- ☐ sex or sexual advances toward a minor
- ☐ inappropriate touching
- ☐ prostitution

Finding what God's doing and following Him there isn't easy when conflict is all up in your face. Especially in a marriage or work situation, the temptation to just react from your flesh or strongholds is intense.

And even if you remain calm and self-controlled, reasoning with that person who's yelling at you may not be possible.

So, one of the things God has taught me to do is

† **Stay silent.** When the person winds down some, explain you need time to pray about what they've said. Then **set an appointment to talk together**, and start that meeting with **prayer, inviting God to guide your conversation** and show you both what He wants to say and do.

Of course, sometimes if you do that, angry people will just get angrier. Rather than agree to a meeting, they might set out on a rampage, avoid you, or talk behind your back, which they were likely to do anyway.

But *most Christians really do want to have loving relationships where God is in control.* They agree to the meeting, and when you ask God to lead your conversation, *He does.* You listen to each other, purpose to understand each other, and pray for each other, as He **completely transforms that situation,** *and especially your hearts!*

> IS THERE SOMEONE YOU NEED TO SET UP A MEETING WITH TO TALK ABOUT A SENSITIVE SUBJECT? ASK GOD TO GUIDE YOU AND TO BE LORD OVER THAT CONVERSATION.
>
> START THAT MEETING WITH PRAYER TOGETHER, INVITING GOD TO GUIDE YOUR THOUGHTS AND WORDS AND HELP YOU UNDERSTAND EACH OTHER.
>
> WRITE IN YOUR JOURNAL WHAT GOD DOES.

Seek God's instructions

Victory strategy 82

Hebrews 13:17; Isaiah 30:15; Proverbs 3:5-7; Romans 13:9

Whatever conflict you're in, God has peace awaiting you in His instructions. But you must seek Him first.

One supervisor who seldom prayed before making decisions* often blocked me from obeying God. When I asked the Lord about it, He said to my heart, "You are My double agent. He just *thinks* you work for him. But really you work for Me. You are My agent of *love*."

What an answer! His gentle words gave me peace and even made me laugh. But I still didn't understand how to be that "double agent" without disobeying someone. So I asked Him for more instructions. Once again, He answered clearly, "Whatever he tells you to do, even if it seems contrary to what I've called you to, say, 'Sure. I can do that. I'm just here to serve.' Then trust Me."

So I did. In each situation, God miraculously opened a loophole for me to slip through to obey Him *without disobeying my leader*. I was so in awe of the Lord those days, I began calling Him "Lord of the Loopholes."

But under another controlling leader, God gave me different instructions. Each time the man's orders blocked obedience to God, I was to reply, "I'll pray about that," and share with him what I felt God saying. Eventually, he humbly told me God had convicted him that he should pray before telling people what to do.

Ex. 20:1-21; Matt. 15:19; Rom. 1:25 ...

- ☐ sex or oral sex outside of marriage
- ☐ inviting or freely allowing someone who is not my husband to touch me in a sexual manner
- ☐ emotional affair
- ☐ sensuality
- ☐ pornography
- ☐ promiscuity
- ☐ uncontrollable desires, passions, and actions
- ☐ hiring a male prostitute

> THE BEST WAY TO FIND WHAT GOD IS DOING IN YOUR TRIAL AND JOIN HIM THERE IS TO ASK HIM. IF YOU'RE STILL HAVING TROUBLE HEARING HIS VOICE, REMEMBER HE'S MORE INTERESTED IN YOUR HEART THAN IN HOW WELL YOU THINK YOU HEAR HIM. JUST SURRENDER, AND THEN HEAD DOWN THE MOST LOVING PATH. HE'LL SHUT THE DOOR IF IT'S NOT THE RIGHT ONE.

---

* For more on the New Testament leadership model of Christ as the Head, read *Dare to Become a Kingdom Culture Leader, Volumes 1-2*, at www.MoreThanAConquerorBooks.com.

Victory Strategy 83: Reject what's not from God

Matthew 7:1-5; 1 John 1:5-9; Psalm 139:23-24

Ex. 20:1-21;
Matt. 15:19;
Rom. 1:25 ...
- [ ] *reading sexual scenes in novels, magazines*
- [ ] *watching sexual scenes on TV or other media*
- [ ] *abnormal desire for sex*
- [ ] *exposure of private parts to a man not my husband (or woman with lesbian intentions)*
- [ ] *uncontrollable desires, actions, passions*
- [ ] *animalistic sex*
- [ ] *immorality*
- [ ] *lasciviousness*
- [ ] *licentiousness*
- [ ] *indecent acts*
- [ ] *preoccupied with sex*
- [ ] *abnormal sex*
- [ ] _____
- [ ] _____

I grew up in a Christian home with encouraging parents. Whenever I followed their instructions on how to do something better, it *was* better. *Their wise advice gave me a genuine love for constructive criticism.*

But when I headed out into the real world, I found most people criticize what they don't understand or what makes them feel uncomfortable. They attack from out of their own pride, judgment, insecurities, wrong thought processes, or painful experiences, not from a genuine desire to mentor or help.

Christians who pick at the splinter in your eye often believe their word is from God. But **hurt people hurt people.** And those who walk around with "judgment logs" may unknowingly deliver a word from the enemy, or twist a word from God through the filters of their strongholds. Matthew 7:1-5.

To clear out the junk and hear only what God is saying,

† **Don't just receive what others say.** Respond, "I'll pray about that," and then **hand their advice, accusations, suggestions, opinions, etc., over to the Lord, asking Him to filter anything out that's not from Him and speak His truth to your heart.**

† **Run their words through the Three-Fold Sieve** (Strategy 12). *Make sure you don't receive anything that is not from God.*

> HAVE YOU RECEIVED A FALSE WORD? OR HAVE YOU TAKEN SOMEONE'S ADVICE TO CHANGE SOMETHING IN YOUR LIFE GOD NEVER ASKED YOU TO CHANGE? ASK THE LORD, AND JOURNAL WHAT HE SHOWS YOU.

Lord, how do You see me?

Judges 6:1-16; John 8:42-47; James 2:19; 4:7-8

Victory Strategy 84

Has the enemy bullied you so long with his lies, it's hard to believe what God says about you is true?

One day, I crawled into my quiet time exhausted and battle weary from all the attacks others had launched against me. I closed my eyes and asked the Lord, "Jesus, when You look at me, what do You see?"

Immediately, a picture came to mind of a little child running up the steps of His throne, tossing off my dinked armor, and crawling up into His lap.

I laughed. That was *precisely* how I felt. Small. Beaten up. But so happy to throw off my burden and let Him hold me.

"Now ask Me how your *enemy* sees you," He whispered into my heart.

The picture changed: I *towered* over the enemy, fully armored — a fearsome giant in Love's power. The demons trembled and *ran*.

What? The *enemy* was the one who felt powerful to me, *not me*. I certainly didn't feel "fearsome." Not in any way.

But that's the problem. I had been seeing what Satan wanted me to see, not what God says is true. **When we stand in Love's power, demons tremble at the sight of Him in us.** Romans 8:31-39, James 2:19, 1 John 4:18.

Often my self-viewpoint is clouded with insecurities; or even the opposite, like convincing myself I'm strong when I'm really not. But when I ask the Lord, "How do You see me?" **His glorious, holy viewpoint cuts through all the film and shows me who I truly am.**

You only have one life, mighty warrior. *Live looking through the eyes of the One Who knows you better than you know yourself.*

> ASK THE LORD OFTEN, "WHEN YOU LOOK AT ME, WHAT DO YOU SEE?" DON'T WORRY IF YOU CAN'T SEE PICTURES. HE OFTEN JUST GIVES ME A VERSE, OR SHOWS ME HOW I'M GRIEVING WHEN I THINK I'M NOT, ETC.

1 Corinthians 6:12-19; 2 Timothy 3:1-9; 1 John 2:16

- ☐ letting sin master me
- ☐ defiling or misusing God's temple; not honoring God with my body
- ☐ lust of flesh
- ☐ lust of eyes
- ☐ pride of life
- ☐ lover of pleasure more than God
- ☐ having a form of Godliness but denying its power
- ☐ _____
- ☐ _____

Victory Strategy 85: "If this is the enemy, stop it!"

1 Peter 5:8-9; Matthew 10:1; Luke 10:19; John 14:12

1 Timothy 5:1-2; 1 Corinthians 6:12-20

- ☐ impure thoughts
- ☐ indulging in sexual fantasies
- ☐ seduction
- ☐ inappropriate touching
- ☐ wearing revealing clothing
- ☐ kissing someone God hasn't given me to marry
- ☐ excessive flirting
- ☐ obsession with orgasm
- ☐ debauchery
- ☐ sexual immorality
- ☐ indecency
- ☐ _____
- ☐ _____
- ☐ _____
- ☐ _____
- ☐ _____
- ☐ _____
- ☐ _____
- ☐ _____

As I wrote that story in Strategy 84, the washing machine broke and flooded. Then I got a text saying, due to anti-terrorism laws, the phone company was going to cut off my phone (I'm an expat living in a closed country).

Coincidence? Not likely. Because after I cleaned up the mess, called the repairman, prayed with my husband about those and other matters, and headed over to the phone company, *fear and discouragement accosted me.*

I said under my breath, "If this is the enemy, stop it in the name of Jesus!" And then I prayed one-by-one for the lost people who passed me, all of whom probably have never heard of Jesus. The fear and discouragement fled, as love, faith, and eternal purposes pushed them out.

I've found many times when I use this tactic, the battle stops immediately. For example, say the tension rises in a conversation. While the person is still speaking, I casually put my hand over my mouth and say in a voice she can't hear but my enemy can:

✝ **"If this is the enemy, stop it! In the name of Jesus!"**

Suddenly, that negative tone calms down and moves on to a pleasant subject. Why? Because **I'm a daughter of the Most High, and** *the same authority Jesus walked in while here on earth He has given to me.* Luke 10:19.

Of course, it doesn't always happen like that. Sometimes Satan feels invited somehow, and puts up quite a fight. But probably 80 percent of the time, speaking out that sentence has turned the battle around, thanks to the power of Christ.

> WHEN ACCIDENTS HAPPEN, ARGUMENTS START, TENSIONS RISE, SOMETHING BLOCKS YOU FROM OBEYING GOD, SOMEONE MAKES SEXUAL ADVANCES TOWARD YOU, NEGATIVE THOUGHTS FILL YOUR MIND, ETC., TRY SAYING, "IF THIS IS THE ENEMY, STOP IT IN THE NAME OF JESUS." THEN PRAY FOR THAT PERSON OR SITUATION.

Pray for eternal things

Victory strategy 86

2 Corinthians 4:7-18; 1 Corinthians 16:13-14; Colossians 3:1-4

In that last story, did you notice I **prayed for the lost,** and as I did, ***the Spirit's power filled me immediately, and the enemy fled?***

This is what I call *going on the offensive* (Strategy 87). Many times, Satan uses broken appliances, sickness, fear, etc., to distract us from eternal matters. But **when we use trials as a reminder to pray for eternal things, the enemy loses more ground by attacking us than not**.

When my toddler was sick with stomach issues for more than two weeks, I prayed day and night for her healing, but she only got worse. A friend dropped by, and when I shared with her what was going on, she said, "Whenever I get headaches, I use them as a reminder to pray for Algeria."

Sometimes a trial persists, even when you pray, because God wants to do something in you. Well, this time, He wanted to teach me a major spiritual warfare tactic.

So, the next time my daughter climbed into my lap, saying, "My tummy hurts," I prayed, "Lord, please heal her," and then launched into deep intercessory prayer for the unreached people group God has called us to. By the next morning, she was *completely healed*.

Healing is most certainly something Jesus is all about. And it's important to pray for protection over your family and things, as well. But ***worrying with your eyes closed*** (like I was doing) ***is not praying in faith.***

Believe that God is in charge, surrender the matter into His hands, and then trust Him with the outcome, *even if it's not what you want Him to do.* Then you can move on to interceding for eternal things — not just because you want the enemy to quit — but *because you love God and those people, and you want to see His kingdom come.* Matthew 22:37-40.

Love is the motive for all things Kingdom Culture, after all. 1 Corinthians 16:14.

Revelation 2:14-16; Deuteronomy 4:2
- [ ] false teaching
- [ ] adding to Scripture what God has not said or twisting it to fit my agenda
- [ ] subtracting from, ignoring or denying Scripture that disagrees with my agenda
- [ ] _____
- [ ] _____
- [ ] _____
- [ ] _____
- [ ] _____

> IS THERE A PERSISTENT SITUATION YOU PRAY FOR BUT SEE NO CHANGE? LEAVE IT IN GOD'S HANDS, AND THEN PRAY ALL THE MORE FOR ETERNAL THINGS.

87 Victory strategy

Offensive strategy
1 Corinthians 6:18; 10:13; Ephesians 6:10-18

(This list below of occult activities goes with Strategy 92. Please mark anything anyone in your family has been involved in, and write notes in the margin.)

1 Samuel 15:23
- ☐ rebellion against God
- ☐ arrogance
- ☐ divination
- ☐ witchcraft
- ☐ sorcery
- ☐ occult activity
- ☐ idolatry
- ☐ Satan worship
- ☐ curses
- ☐ black magic, arts
- ☐ black mass
- ☐ white magic
- ☐ neutral magic
- ☐ séances
- ☐ clairvoyance
- ☐ mediums
- ☐ divining
- ☐ psychic powers
- ☐ spiritism
- ☐ necromancy
- ☐ conjuring spirits
- ☐ fortune-telling
- ☐ trance diagnosis

As my husband and I led worship at church, one man who helped us seemed attracted to me. I didn't think anything of it, because he was about 10-15 years younger and married, but every time we worshiped together, there was that feeling again. It was distracting, to say the least.

By the third Sunday that happened, I finally said under my breath, "If this is the enemy, stop it," and then began praying for his freedom. The man had no idea what I was doing, of course, and I have no idea what God did in his heart, but *never again did he flirt with me or look at me in a lustful way.*

† This strategy of **standing in God's power and love, in the midst of attack, to intercede for freedom, salvation, or other eternal matters** deals Satan's armies a crippling offensive blow.

Sometimes, however, the spiritual issue could be your own. If you have a sexual stronghold, for example, and that other person has one too, then the enemy could be having quite a party in the air. No matter how strong the attraction to sin, **God has promised you a way of escape, so look for it and *take* it.** 1 Corinthians 10:13.

> IF SATAN IS USING OTHERS TO GET AT YOU, WHETHER THROUGH SEXUAL TEMPTATION, ANGER, ACCUSATION, MIND-READING OR ANYTHING ELSE, TRY PRAYING IN THE MIDST OF THAT ATTACK FOR THEIR FREEDOM. THEN CONTINUE TO PRAY FOR THEM AFTERWARDS, WHENEVER GOD BRINGS THEM TO MIND.

Break soul ties

1 Corinthians 6:12-20; Matthew 5:27-28; Genesis 2:22-24

Victory Strategy 88

Take a moment to look at the checklist for sexual sins and wrong thought processes on pages 89-94.

Have you ever been in an intimate relationship outside of marriage? Have you ever been molested or sexually abused in any way? Have you ever had sexual thoughts or fantasies about someone who is not your husband? Have you ever exposed your private parts, whether in person, through social media, or some other sexual way? Have you allowed someone who is not your husband to sexually touch, kiss, or caress you? Have you thought about it?

If so, according to 1 Corinthians 6:12-20 and Matthew 5:27-28, you have bound yourself "as one" to that person — a union reserved *only for marriage* — and you have used God's temple for unholy acts.

Like any sin, Jesus is standing here loving you, ready with His grace. Ask forgiveness, and receive His cleansing. Let Him transform you through a Truth Encounter (Strategy 18), and give you instructions to walk in freedom. His sacrifice has made you perfect, without blemish. Now, you're in the process of being made holy. Hebrews 10:14.

1 Sam. 15:23 ...
- ☐ palm reading
- ☐ tea-leaf reading
- ☐ crystal balls
- ☐ casting spells
- ☐ astrology
- ☐ Moon-many horoscopes
- ☐ zodiac signs
- ☐ icons
- ☐ numerology
- ☐ parapsychology
- ☐ enchantments
- ☐ clairaudience
- ☐ unholy dreams
- ☐ unholy visions
- ☐ fetishes
- ☐ runes
- ☐ amulets
- ☐ talismans
- ☐ mascots
- ☐ ankhs

> TO REPENT AND CUT OFF UNHOLY TIES, PRAY SOMETHING LIKE THE PRAYER BELOW, AND THEN DO WHATEVER ELSE THE LORD ASKS YOU TO.

"Lord forgive me for _____ (sin, thought, act). In the name of Jesus, I break any unholy ties to _____ (name), and I bless him (her) and his (her) marriage to be founded on You, for You alone are True Love. If anything unholy has passed to me from him (her) or from him (her) to me, I cut that off now in Your name, Jesus, and I ask You to redeem whatever was lost in that unholy union. Set me free from the thought processes that lead me in wrong directions, and set me apart for the one You have chosen for me to marry. Teach me how to remain pure and led by Your Spirit in all my choices and thoughts. Help me be the woman of God you created me to be as a sister to my brothers and sisters and as a wife to my husband."

89 Victory Strategy: Build protective hedges

James 1:13-15

1 Sam. 15:23 ...

- ☐ unholy medals
- ☐ spells
- ☐ incantations
- ☐ potions
- ☐ acupuncture
- ☐ mysticism
- ☐ Aryanism
- ☐ Humanism
- ☐ psycho-kinesis
- ☐ telepathy
- ☐ psychometry
- ☐ mind control
- ☐ second sight
- ☐ mental science
- ☐ self-realization
- ☐ visualization
- ☐ trances
- ☐ yoga
- ☐ mesmerism
- ☐ auras
- ☐ reincarnation
- ☐ psycho-analysis
- ☐ wizards
- ☐ soothsaying
- ☐ prostitution
- ☐ prognosticators
- ☐ psychography
- ☐ transference
- ☐ New Age
- ☐ powwow
- ☐ yin-yang
- ☐ superstition
- ☐ spiritualism
- ☐ occult literature

What draws you into doing or thinking what you know you shouldn't?

While you're still seeking the Lord for freedom from your strongholds, if there's any way to stop putting yourself in situations that tempt you, then *do it!*

For example, if you know you're attracted to a certain man (or woman), purpose to stay away from the places where he frequents, or make sure you only go there under your husband's arm. If he calls you or texts you, include your husband in the chat. Or block the man's calls altogether.

Whether your struggle is food, internet, entertainment, drugs, alcohol, sexual issues, impatience, depression, or anything else, having an **accountability partner** you can be real with is a great way to stand strong. She can listen to your heart, pray for you, challenge you, and also help reinforce whatever instructions God is giving you to walk in freedom.

> SEEK THE LORD FOR HIS PERFECT PLAN TO PROTECT YOU FROM TEMPTATION. ASK HIM FOR INSTRUCTIONS ON HOW TO BUILD A WIDE WALL AROUND THE SINS THAT TEMPT YOU SO YOU WON'T GO ANYWHERE NEAR THEM. WRITE IN YOUR JOURNAL WHAT HE SHOWS YOU, AND THEN WALK OUT IN HIS PLAN.
>
> IS THERE ANYONE HE IS LEADING YOU TO FOR A PRAYER PARTNER OR ACCOUNTABILITY PARTNER?

Cloak of transparency

Genesis 20:3-6; Isaiah 59:12-16; Psalm 112:2

Victory strategy 90

1 Sam. 15:23 ...
- [ ] the force
- [ ] holistic medicine
- [ ] graven images
- [ ] idolatry
- [ ] planchette
- [ ] horoscopes
- [ ] witchcraft, sorcery
- [ ] precognition
- [ ] soul travel
- [ ] eckankar
- [ ] offerings to spirits
- [ ] table tipping
- [ ] good luck charms
- [ ] incense
- [ ] automatic writing
- [ ] Masters of Wisdom
- [ ] apparitions
- [ ] ghosts
- [ ] E.S.P.
- [ ] mind reading
- [ ] poltergeists
- [ ] blood pacts

My friend had a dream one night that the enemy was chasing her, but he couldn't find her because she was transparent. Even when he was only a few feet away and looking straight in her direction, he could only see the trees behind her.

What a powerful visual of how God shields us from the enemy when we're transparent. **You see, whatever we hold in secret the enemy can use against us.**

You know what I'm talking about. We've all had secret sins or places our minds hang out that we'd rather no one know about. But sweeping our dirt under the rug doesn't make it go away. We need to be transparent with God, and tell Him what's going on in our hearts so He can set us free.

And we also need to be transparent with our brothers and sisters. I'm not suggesting that you throw your dirty laundry out there for everyone to smell. But do you have someone you can trust? Someone who will pray with you, help hold you accountable, encourage you, challenge you, and speak truth to you?

Many times, when I have struggled in my thought life and have shared with someone I trust who will love me and pray with me, *the battle goes away immediately.* Other times, it takes a little longer, but having the body of Christ around me to encourage and challenge me made all the difference.

Is there an area of your thought life you've been hiding in darkness? How has the enemy thrived there?

Share those thoughts with the Lord today, ask Him what He thinks, and let Him lead you to someone you can confide in who will pray for you, encourage you, and help you to freedom.

Victory Strategy 91

Don't cause others to fall
Matthew 5:27-30; 18:6; 1 Corinthians 10:23-33

1 Sam. 15:23 ...
- ☐ Magic Eight Ball
- ☐ Christian Science
- ☐ channeling spirits
- ☐ occult movies or TV shows
- ☐ spiritual prostitution
- ☐ wart or bum charming
- ☐ humanistic psychology
- ☐ holographic images
- ☐ out-of-body experience
- ☐ animism, spirit worship
- ☐ The Way International
- ☐ Unification Church
- ☐ Jehovah's Witnesses
- ☐ Science of the Mind
- ☐ Freemasonry (Masons)
- ☐ Swedenborgianism
- ☐ Silva Mind Control
- ☐ Theosophical Society
- ☐ Eastern religions
- ☐ Order of the Arrow
- ☐ levitation

What isn't an issue for you may very well be one for someone else. You may think it's okay to drink alcohol, but if your sister feels tempted by it, then don't drink around her, especially if she is a recovering alcoholic.

In all things, **let Love guide your thoughts and actions.** Matthew 22:37-40.

In the same way, please be careful what you wear. Men are turned on by sexy clothes that are clingy, see-through or show a bit of skin. Check a shirt before you buy it to make sure it doesn't gap when you lean over, so men can't see your breasts. I have actually sewn tank tops high enough onto my bras so they don't move around or expose my chest, even when I bend over. Wearing those modified bras under my clothes has made a huge difference in where men's eyes wander when they look at me.

Don't let style make your decisions for you. If those shorts are too short, or that shirt too low, don't buy it and don't wear it. Ask God to lead you to the clothes that compliment the beauty He has endowed you with but won't lead your brother's thoughts astray.

Because when he's even just thought about you in a lustful way, he's already fallen, Jesus said. Matthew 5:27-30.

Don't let the enemy use you in someone else's life. *Love your brother more*; your vanity just isn't worth his fall.

> ASK GOD IF THERE'S ANYTHING YOU'RE DOING THAT MIGHT CAUSE OTHERS TO THINK THOUGHTS THEY SHOULDN'T OR FEEL TEMPTED TO DO SOMETHING GOD HAS ASKED THEM NOT TO. THEN SEEK HIM FOR INSTRUCTIONS ON HOW TO CHANGE THAT.
>
> **WHETHER YOU DRINK, DRESS, SPEAK, OR ACT, LET EVERYTHING YOU DO BE DONE IN LOVE.**

Renounce occult activity

Leviticus 20:6-7, 26; Galatians 5:16-25; Matthew 18:18

Victory Strategy 92

Sin, witchcraft, and idolatry affect not only the sinner, but the whole family, even for generations to come. Deuteronomy 5:7-8, Exodus 20:5. (See also Deuteronomy 18:9-14; 2 Timothy 3:8; Leviticus 19:26, 31; 20:6, 27; 1 Chronicles 10:13-14; 2 Kings 21:5-6, 19-20; Isaiah 2:6, 8-19; Jeremiah 27:9-10; Zechariah 10:2.)

When we engage in occult activity, however innocent we feel the situation is, we invite Satan to speak to us, welcoming him into our home and giving him access to our lives and families. *He must be uninvited.*

Even if the occult activity happened through someone else in the family or before your conversion, you need to close that door by confessing and renouncing it. Judges 10:15, 1 Samuel 12:10, Ezekiel 14:6.

My children and I suffered from a genetic blood disease, as well as recurring respiratory illnesses. In my quiet times, I felt God urging me to cut off any curses through my grandfathers' and great grandfather's Freemasonry vows, and when I obeyed Him, *we were healed.* John 14:13-15.

1 Sam. 15:23 ...
- [ ] death wishes, oaths
- [ ] psychic involvement
- [ ] psycho-cybernetics
- [ ] letters of protection
- [ ] mental suggestion
- [ ] Umbanda, Macumba
- [ ] psychic phenomena
- [ ] metaphysical healing
- [ ] hypnosis, self-hypnosis
- [ ] transcendental meditation
- [ ] E.S.T. (The Forum)
- [ ] transactional analysis
- [ ] self-help techniques

> PRAY THROUGH THE LIST OF OCCULT ACTIVITIES IN THE RUNNING CHECKLIST ON PAGES 96-108, AND CHECK THOSE SOMEONE IN YOUR FAMILY OR EXTENDED FAMILY HAS BEEN INVOLVED IN. WRITE THE CONNECTION IN THE MARGIN. THEN PRAY A PRAYER SIMILAR TO THE ONE BELOW.

"Lord, please forgive (me, my father, my mother, my grandfather, my uncle, etc.) for (occult activity). (On behalf of my forefathers), I renounce (occult activity). I turn my back on it and I choose to follow only You, Jesus. Break every curse, influence, or demonic scheme from off of me, my family, my children, and my children's children forever. In the name of Jesus, I send the spirit of death and any other spirits assigned to our family (name them, if you know who they are) to the feet of Jesus now to be dealt with by Him, and I forbid them to return. Jesus, I ask You to be a Shield around our family, protecting us from enemy assaults, and turning every curse into a blessing...."

93 Victory Strategy

"Go! And don't come back!"
Matthew 8:16, 32; 10:1; Mark 9:14-29

1 Sam. 15:23 ...

- ☐ esoteric philosophy
- ☐ self-mutilation
- ☐ Karma
- ☐ Buddhism
- ☐ Islam
- ☐ Black Muslim
- ☐ Hinduism
- ☐ Taosim
- ☐ Unity
- ☐ Mormonism
- ☐ omens
- ☐ occult jewelry
- ☐ yoga
- ☐ Bahaism
- ☐ magic healing
- ☐ Eastern Star
- ☐ Hare Krishna
- ☐ hypnotherapy
- ☐ Roy Masters
- ☐ Father Divine
- ☐ shrines, temples
- ☐ lodges
- ☐ imaginary friend
- ☐ oaths
- ☐ false cults
- ☐ rock music
- ☐ martial arts
- ☐ evil dance
- ☐ voodoo
- ☐ thought control
- ☐ tattooing
- ☐ cutting the body

Jesus is our Model in all things, and **He has given us His authority** regarding spiritual matters. Luke 10:19, John 14:12. Did you notice that in that prayer in Strategy 92 we commanded the demons to go and not come back? That's because in Matthew 8:16, Jesus sent the demons away with a word, and verse 32 tells us that word is _____. In Mark 9:25, we see Him commanding a demon to go and never return.

We're not supposed to just stand around in our armor looking pretty. *This is all-out war!* Ephesians 6:10-20, John 5:19.

If you have a family member suffering from

- schizophrenia or other mental illness
- suicidal thoughts or murderous thoughts
- a strong compulsion to fall asleep or run out of the room when God is speaking through someone or through His Word
- demonic visitations
- hearing voices
- freak accidents, unexplained illnesses, early death
- death to relationships, death to ministry, etc.

it's possible there is an open door to the enemy through occult activity, and that a spirit of death (among other demonic influences) is at work. But even if you don't see those symptoms in your family, it is still wise to slam the door shut on occult activity.

And if you have a family member who is actively involved in the occult, you will want to pray prayers of protection and cleansing often.

Did you notice that *rebellion* and *arrogance* are at the beginning of the list of occult involvement on page 96? Why? 1 Samuel 15:23. _____

> ASK THE LORD WHAT EVIL FORCES ARE AT WORK AGAINST YOU AND YOUR FAMILY, AND FOLLOW HIS LEAD IN DISINVITING THEM.

Cleanse your home

Acts 19:18-20; Deuteronomy 7:25-26; Isaiah 60:18b

Victory strategy 94

1 Sam. 15:23 ...
- ☐ *graphology*
- ☐ *neo-rationalism*
- ☐ *agnosticism*
- ☐ *atheism*
- ☐ *reflexology*
- ☐ *color therapy*
- ☐ *death magic*
- ☐ *firewalking*
- ☐ *fanaticism*
- ☐ *Rosicrucianism*
- ☐ *screening*
- ☐ *mind science*
- ☐ *autosuggestion*
- ☐ *biofeedback*
- ☐ *psychic healing*
- ☐ *inner voices*
- ☐ *Children of God*
- ☐ *tarot cards or other card laying*
- ☐ *observing of the times*
- ☐ *astral projection*

Sometimes the enemy feels he has rights to afflict a household because of a previous tenant's occult activity or unholy acts in that location. For example, a child in a Christian home suffered from terrible nightmares and demonic visitations. When the family discovered her room had been used for spirit worship by a former tenant, they "cleansed" it with prayer and worship, and the affliction stopped.

If you have articles associated with occult practices, idolatry, or spirit worship in your home (even if it is just a souvenir from a trip), you will want to get rid of those by destroying them, throwing them out, or praying cleansing prayers over them, as God leads.

But even if you don't know if the above situations are true of your house or not, take time to pray through your home and worship, blessing each room and dedicating it to the Lord. Ask Him to send anything out that's not of Him and to fill it with His presence and His angels.

This is a wonderful activity to do as a family. In fact, your children will enjoy writing verses around the house as He leads. Zechariah 14:20-21. Our family does this often, and especially when we travel. Whatever hotel room or home we stay in, we pray a cleansing prayer like this one below, to sleep peacefully under God's protection.

"In the name of Jesus, we declare we are the current occupants of this room, and Jesus is our King, so He rules here. In the name of Jesus, we cancel any enemy rights to this place because of previous evil acts. Whatever is in this room that is not of the Lord, we cast it out in the name of Jesus, and we ask You, God, to fill this room with Your presence. Be a shield around this home and the glory within. Zechariah 2:5. Fill this place so full of Your glory, Your presence, and Your love, that when people walk into our home, they will walk into You...."

> SPEND TIME "CLEANING HOUSE" TODAY. ASK GOD IF THERE ARE ANY ARTICLES YOU NEED TO GET RID OF, AND OBEY HIM. THEN WORSHIP THROUGH YOUR HOME, ASKING HIM TO FILL IT WITH HIS PRESENCE AND DEDICATING EVERY ROOM AND PERSON TO HIM.

95 Victory Strategy — Break generational curses

Exodus 34:6-7; Psalm 79:8; Proverbs 28:13; Nehemiah 1:1-11

1 Sam. 15:23 ...

- ☐ vows (Js. 5:12; Matt. 5:34-37)
- ☐ concept therapy
- ☐ human or animal sacrifice
- ☐ materialization or apports
- ☐ contact with familiar spirits
- ☐ communicating with dead
- ☐ pact with Satan
- ☐ spirit rod or pendulum diagnosis
- ☐ consulting spirit guides, mediums
- ☐ automatic drawing or composing
- ☐ massage by someone who channels spirits
- ☐ dedication to a spirit, to Satan or to a cult
- ☐ consciousness-expanding through drugs
- ☐ Science of Creative Intelligence

Are there issues in your life that feel as if they've always been there? Do others in your family struggle with the same thing?

Generational ties to sin or recurring difficulties are nothing new. The Bible gives many accounts of children, grandchildren, and yet more generations walking in the same sins or hardships as their forefathers. 1 Kings 15:3, 26; 22:52, etc.

Although we have a tendency to imitate what our parents model, there is also a spiritual aspect. When we listen to the enemy's lies and receive them by sinning or giving in to the thought directions Satan leads us in, we are essentially opening the door and inviting him and his cohorts in to hang out and speak into our lives. And once they feel invited, they may feel they have the right to bother others in our family with the same lies, sins, assaults and temptations.

> ASK GOD TO SHOW YOU ANY GENERATIONAL STRONGHOLDS OR CURSES. THEN CLOSE THAT DOOR HOWEVER HE LEADS. HERE ARE SOME BEGINNING STEPS (I'LL USE ANGER AS AN EXAMPLE.):

- **Forgive** the one who opened the door to (anger).
- **Repent** from your own (anger) or involvement in it.
- Seek God for a **Truth Encounter** (Strategy 18) for freedom from lies that lead you personally to (anger).
- Declare something like, *"In the name of Jesus, and on behalf of (my forefather), I shut the door on (anger), and I break any curses associated with it. I forbid (anger) to ever pick on me, my children, my children's children, or anyone in my family ever again. And I send (anger) and any demonic forces associated with it to the feet of Jesus to be dealt with by Him. Jesus, I ask You to be a Shield around me and my family to keep us from evil attacks. Fill us with Your (love), (grace), (mercy), (gentleness), (kindness), and (joy). Wash our family line clean of (anger), and fill us with the whole measure of the fullness of Christ. Trample all enemy plans against me and my family, and bring forth Your purposes in us. In Your name. Amen."*

Free your children to be free

Victory strategy 96

Genesis 20:3-6; Isaiah 59:9-21; Psalm 112:2

As my toddlers played together one day, I suddenly heard, "Mine! Mine!" It wasn't normal for them to argue over a toy, so I asked the Lord what was going on.

He pointed His gentle finger at greed in my own heart, and I repented right there on the spot. Then I said in a voice the children couldn't hear but my enemy could, "Greed, get out of this house! You're not welcome here!"

The arguing stopped *immediately*.

After such a clear illustration from the Lord, I began diligently opening my heart to Him every day in my quiet times so He could transform me.

With every stronghold He set me free from, I saw a marked difference in my children, as well.

But when they reached a certain age, it wasn't enough for me to repent and cut off the enemy from whatever rights he felt he had to pick on our family; my kids had to repent too.

For my son, it was around age five, the same year he chose to follow Christ. Broken over his sin and standing in his own authority in Christ, he said no to the enemy's plans on his life and grew up to be a man after God's own heart.

> HAVE YOU WELCOMED ANYTHING INTO YOUR HOME YOU NEED TO DISINVITE? ASK GOD, AND THEN WRITE A PRAYER IN YOUR JOURNAL SHUTTING THAT DOOR.

1 Sam. 15:23 ...
- ☐ charts with occult significance
- ☐ mental manipulation,
- ☐ mind-swapping
- ☐ ancestor worship or veneration
- ☐ fortune-telling or anything that predicts my future and has advised my life
- ☐ blood subscriptions (subscribing myself or my children to the devil)
- ☐ false or demonic tongues (test by 1 Jn. 4:1-3 and 1 Cor. 12:3)

97 Victory Strategy

Pray in your authority

John 15:7; Matthew 18:20; 1 Corinthians 11:1-15

1 Sam. 15:23 ...

- ☐ association with or possession of occult or pagan objects, relics, idols, images, artifacts or anything that has been dedicated to spirits
- ☐ religion or philosophy that denies the deity or blood atonement of Jesus (liberal theology that teaches salvation without repentance, Modem Theology, rationalistic or intellectual theology that denies the resurrection, the second coming, miracles, answers to prayer, spiritual gifts, the devil, demons, or God)
- ☐ remote influence of the subconscious mind of others
- ☐ iridology

As sons and daughters of the Most High, we are joint heirs with Christ in His Kingdom. *That's why the enemy is so afraid of us when we pray together for the things of His heart.* John 15:7, Matthew 18:20.

One day in my quiet time I asked the Lord, "Why have You blessed me so much?" He answered, "Never underestimate the power of praying parents."

What a word! As parents, we have special authority in the spiritual realm to cover our children in prayer.

In the same way, a pastor can cover his congregation, a leader his team, and a husband his wife when he prays in the authority God has given him.

For this reason, whenever I do ministry, I seek my husband and others to cover me in prayer. And we often add single women into our daily family prayers for protection.

But even as my sister in Christ, you have so much authority in the spiritual realm to pray for me and see healing and other breakthroughs happen in my life, because we're both daughters of the King together as one under His covering.

Another interesting thing I've noticed about spiritual authority is, whenever my husband left for a ministry trip, things often went wrong — car wrecks, illnesses, hospital stays, broken appliances. But whenever he asked a Godly man or couple in town to cover our family in prayer during his absence, things went much smoother.

I'm still learning about prayer and authority in the spiritual realm, but I've found *the closer I walk with Christ, the more powerfully God works through my prayers.* John 15:7.

> WHOM HAS GOD PLACED UNDER YOUR COVERING? HOW DO YOU FEEL GOD LEADING YOU TO PRAY FOR THEM?
>
> IS THERE A SITUATION THAT MIGHT BENEFIT FROM SEVERAL OF YOU JOINING TOGETHER IN PRAYER? ASK THE LORD AND STEP OUT IN OBEDIENCE.

Walk in your authority

Genesis 3:16; Ephesians 5:21-33; 1 Corinthians 7:4; Judges 4

Victory Strategy 98

According to Scripture, husbands and fathers have a unique authority over their wives and families.

When I was sick with a disease the doctors called incurable, Christian friends came by and prayed for me, and God lifted the pressure and pain for an hour or so. *But whenever my husband prayed for me, the pain lifted for several hours. I could even sleep!* Eventually, the Lord healed me, a miracle that still leaves us in awe.

Other times, when our family has come under spiritual attack, my husband has taken the lead and prayed for freedom, rest, or victory, and God answered in dramatic ways.

But rarely have I met a man who truly walks in the fullness of his God-given authority, leading his family spiritually, training them up in the Word, and covering them in prayer. More often, he leaves that up to the wife.

If you are in that position, dear woman of God, you still have authority as a wife and mother to pray with your husband and/or for him, and to lead your children to know the Lord, even if he does not participate as you feel he should. There is no Scripture that says you cannot teach your children to follow God.

In fact, in the Word, *when men did not step up to the plate, God handed authority and leadership to women.* Judges 4. Perhaps that is why so many more women are on the mission field today than men.

So, if you find yourself alone in obeying God, walk under as much covering as your earthly husband or Godly leaders can give, but don't be afraid to follow Christ as your Husband. His mantel is wide enough to cover you, even if you are single. Don't let the enemy twist Scripture to prevent you from obeying the Lord. Galatians 3:28. Seek Godly counsel and prayer covering, and ask the Lord for instructions on how to lovingly obey Him. (See my story in Strategy 82.)

1 Sam. 15:23 ...
- ☐ handwriting analysis
- ☐ occult games (Dungeons and Dragons, Clairvoyant, Kabala, Mystic Eye, ESP, Ouija Board, Telepathy, Voodoo, Horoscope, Masters of the Universe, etc.)
- ☐ initiation rites (into lodges, brotherhoods, shrines, clubs, sororities or fraternities that require taking an oath to uphold a man-made doctrine)

> Is there any way you have felt oppressed because of your gender? Seek the Lord for healing (Strategy 18.)

99 Victory strategy

Worship intercession

2 Chronicles 20; Isaiah 30:29-32; Psalm 149

1 Sam. 15:23 ...

☐ radiesthesia (water witching, dowsing forked sticks or other objects to locate water, oil, minerals, underground sewer and water lines, etc.)

☐ incubi and succubae (sexual molestation by an evil spirit)

☐ fantasies, obsessions, or other associations with vampires, draculas, werewolves or other demonic-occultic super-human manifestations

☐ Other: ___
___
___
___
___
___
___

Worship invites God near, and **changes our focus** from how big our problems are to how great our God is. **Worship changes us.**

It's easy for the angels who see God's face every day to worship Him. But when His children down here in this world filled with sin and trials worship in spirit and in truth, sight unseen, from the midst of all our hardships and heartache, that is —

I paused here as I wrote that sentence, looking for the word God wanted, because the picture I saw was of all of Heaven stopping to listen, and tears streaming down the cheeks of the glorious One we love.

"Triumphant" is the word He whispered into my heart.

Worship defeats the enemy. 2 Chronicles 20; Isaiah 30:29-32; Psalm 149. **It blesses, honors, and lifts high the One we love, joining us to His winning side.**

In fact, often in worship, I find the Spirit moving me into powerful intercession to set captives free or pray for nations. Because **worship breaks the chains of the enemy and sends him to flight.** 1 Samuel 16:14-23.

> SPEND TIME WITH THE LORD TODAY SINGING, DANCING, PLAYING AN INSTRUMENT, WRITING HIM A POEM, PAINTING PICTURES FROM YOUR HEART TO HIS, READING A PSALM, OR JUST TELLING HIM HOW MARVELOUS HE IS.
>
> YOU MAY ENJOY MAKING PLAYLISTS OF WORSHIP SONGS THAT FOLLOW THE THEMES GOD'S BEEN TEACHING YOU, AND WORSHIPING TO THOSE.
>
> AS YOU WORSHIP, LET HIM PRESS INTO YOUR HEART SPECIAL PRAYERS OF INTERCESSION FOR THE NATIONS, THE LOST, THE OPPRESSED, AND THOSE WHO NEED FREEDOM.

Be still

Psalm 46:10; Exodus 14:14; Ephesians 6:13

Victory strategy 100

Sometimes, the best strategy against the enemy is simply to *be still*.

Because this battle is about walking as one with Christ and doing whatever He leads and empowers us to do, it's obvious that the enemy would want to keep us busy, distracted, and not taking time to be with the Lord.

So, be still. Enjoy the Lord. Soak in His presence. Listen to His voice. Fall asleep in His arms....

And let Him fight for you. Exodus 14:14.

> One of the main reasons we can't hear the Lord or walk in His empowering is because we don't take the time to be still and know Him.
>
> Today, play some soft worship music in the background, if you like, and just lie still before the Lord, with your heart at rest.
>
> What is He saying to you? Ask Him.
>
> Soak in that word from Him, as He fights off your enemy, while you rest in His presence.

What has God set you free from? Mark those out in this running sidebar.

What is He still working on in you? Pray Philippians 1:6 in faith for each of those strongholds or wrong thought processes.

Review with the Lord all the ways He has transformed your heart and relationships so far. Thank Him. And ask Him for yet more of Him in your life and family.

Deepen your oneness with Christ through these Bible studies, journals, and other books from inspirational author

Mikaela Vincent

MoreThanAConquerorBooks.com

Dare to Become a Kingdom Culture Leader

Volume One: One Passion, One Purpose, One King

Volume Two: Oneness and the Watchman Warrior

Step into the destiny you were created for.

Become a Kingdom Culture Leader.

Whether you're a parent, teacher, pastor, missionary, worship leader, or even just Joe Blow Christian, this Bible study workbook to write in is for you. Through practical lessons on listening to God's voice, making wise decisions, following the Spirit's leading, walking in humility, promoting unity, and leading others well, author Mikaela Vincent uses small group Bible studies that can also be studied as a daily devotional to dig deep into the Bible and form new thought processes and habits so we can walk as one with Christ and lead out as Kingdom Culture influencers.

Dare to Become a Kingdom Culture Leader is based on the New Testament model of the church as the body of Christ, with the Lord as the Head, and offers steps for experiencing God, spiritual warfare, and following Jesus' calling in parenting, pastoring, mentoring and other leadership roles.

Delight to Be a Woman of God

Deep Bible studies for Christian single women today on listening to God's voice, walking in the Spirit, unlocking your beauty, and finding true love, happiness and freedom

Do you long for true love? Are you tired of falling into the same old messes again and again? Do you desire to be truly beautiful? Packed full with tools for hearing God's voice, finding freedom from strongholds and lies, and walking in the Spirit's power, this Bible study guide by Mikaela Vincent will strengthen your faith, transform your mind, and empower you to overcome. A leader's guide is included, but this workbook can also be used for personal devotionals. Recommended for ages 14 and above. For younger women, try *Delight to Become a Woman of God*.

Delight to Be a Woman of God Prayer Journal

This companion to *Delight to Be a Woman of God* is full of tools for recognizing God's voice and walking as one with Him. Available with or without lines.

Delight to Become a Woman of God

30 Bible studies from a mother's heart to her daughter's on drawing near to Christ and loving well

It's not a fairy tale. It's true. You really are a princess, destined to marry the King. And together you'll live happily forever after. It's all you ever dreamed life could be, and it's all yours, if you choose to become a woman of God. This Bible study guide for young women ages 12 and above, offers original illustrations, personal stories, deep questions, and Scripture to point young women to deeper depths with Christ so they can be set free from the things that keep them from the abundant life they were created for. A group study leader's guide is included. But this workbook can also be used for personal quiet times.

Dare to Be a Man of God

Powerful Bible studies for young men today on listening to God's voice and winning life's battles

Pull out your "sword" and get ready for a dive into the Word that just might change your life! This workbook for single men offers practical tools for knowing God's voice, overcoming strongholds, tapping into the Spirit's power, finding the wife your King has chosen for you, and pushing back the darkness. Step into the adventure today, and dare to be a true man of God! A leader's guide is included, but the studies can also be done as private devotionals. We recommend this workbook for any single man 14 years and older. (For younger ages, try *Dare to Become a Man of God*).

Dare to Be a Man of God Prayer Journal

Take this companion to *Dare to Be a Man of God* into your quiet times for some exciting conversations with the King. Packed full with tools for recognizing God's voice and walking as one with Him, this notebook to write in is available with or without lines.

Dare to Become a Man of God

30 Bible studies from a mother's heart to her son's on drawing near to Christ and living victoriously.

Whether you like it or not, you are at war. Will you dare to defy enemy schemes? Will you dare to fight for the things that matter? Will you dare to become a man of God? Cartoons, personal stories, deep questions, practical how-to steps, and Scripture all point youth ages 12 and up to fix their eyes on Jesus and draw near to Him as they fight the good fight, listen to God's voice and make wise decisions through His guidance, so they can become more than conquerors through every tough situation life presents. A leader's guide is included, but this workbook can also be studied as a devotional in personal quiet times.

Pure-As-Gold Children's Books
by Mikaela Vincent
www.MoreThanAConquerorBooks.com
Equipping young hearts today for the battles of tomorrow.

Out You Go, Fear!

Is your child afraid of the night? Does he sometimes "see" monsters in the dark? Does she have nightmares or awake in a panic? Do you? This story about a fearful, but eventually brave boy addresses night fears most children experience. Through colorful pictures, sound truths, and a fun storyline, Vincent offers children ages 4-8 (and parents too!) steps to freedom from fear so they can sleep in peace. Includes tips for parents on helping their children to freedom from nightmares and the effects of traumatic memories.

I Want a Horse

Have you ever wanted something so much it was all you could think of or dream about? In this inspirational picture book for ages 4-8, Mikaela Vincent uses colorful artwork, imaginative poetry and heartwarming humor to tell the story of a young girl who asks for her heart's desire only to discover a treasure she already has that surpasses her imaginations. Moms and daughters will especially enjoy a deep bond reading together this fun interchange between an ambitious little girl and her wise and creative mother.

I Want to See Jesus

This easy-to-read book for ages 3-7 uses colorful drawings and simple words to teach just-beginning readers that Jesus is always with us, even when we can't see Him.

Chronicles of the Kingdom of Light
fantasy with purpose
by Mikaela Vincent

Based on stories created by Mikaela Vincent to help her children live who they are in Christ, some have compared these first two books in the *Chronicles of the Kingdom of Light* to the *Chronicles of Narnia* because of the inspirational allegory filled with adventure, humor, illustrations, and truths that just might change your life, including freedom from fear, lies, and strongholds.

Book 1: Rescue from Darkness

Snatched from their summer fun by a sudden tragedy, six friends loyal to the King of Light embark upon an unforgettable adventure into the Kingdom of Darkness to rescue a young boy held hostage by evil creatures.

Astride such mystical mounts as a winged tiger, a flying unicorn, and a giant cobra, these ordinary young people engage in an extraordinary battle that will cost them more than they counted on. As they struggle against monsters — and even each other — to overcome the fight against night, the friends soon discover the true enemy that must be conquered is the enemy within themselves.

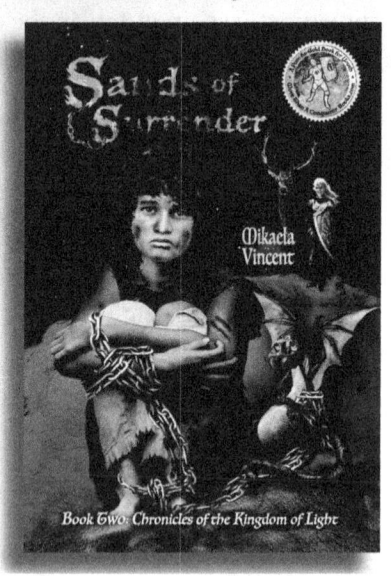

Book 2: Sands of Surrender

Banished by the King of Light, Cory cannot continue the search for his kidnapped brother until he discovers a way back into the Kingdom of Darkness where the boy is held prisoner.

When creatures of Darkness offer to lead him there, his decision to follow costs him his freedom and exposes a plot against his family so dangerous he may not make it out alive.

Meanwhile, Victoria sets out on her own misadventure to rescue her friend, but her decisions place those she loves in such terrible peril, Cory's life is not the only one she must save.

Follow, friend, like Mikaela Vincent, and share with others:

Facebook Page: **Mikaela.Vincent.author**
Facebook Profile: **Mikaela.Vincent.MoreThanAConquerorBooks**
Instagram: **Mikaela.Vincent**
Twitter: **Mikaela_Vincent**
Pinterest: **Mikaela Vincent: More Than A Conqueror Books**
Blog: **www.MoreThanAConquerorBooks.wordpress.com**

Mikaela Vincent serves the Lord with her husband in a dark area of the world where few have ever heard the name of Jesus. Most of her books were written together with the Lord in her quiet times to influence her children and those she mentors to become all God created them to be —

more than conquerors.

All proceeds received by the author go to shining Light in the darkness. If you'd like to know more about how you can help Mikaela and her ministry, or if you have any questions, write

MoreThanAConquerorBooks@gmail.com.

Thank you for being a part of catching the world on fire for the One Who created it for His glory.

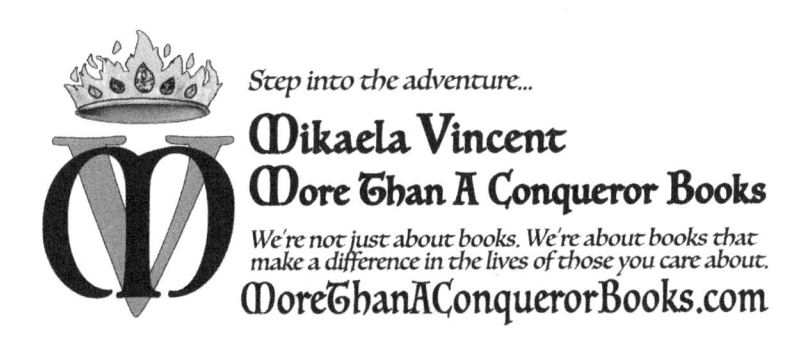

Step into the adventure...

Mikaela Vincent
More Than A Conqueror Books

We're not just about books. We're about books that make a difference in the lives of those you care about.

MoreThanAConquerorBooks.com

Made in the USA
Las Vegas, NV
27 August 2023